Angel On Call

Pathways to Love and Enlightenment

Helene Rothschild, MS, MA, MFT

Robert D. Reed Publishers   Bandon, OR   www.rdrpublishers.com

Robert D. Reed Publishers
P.O. Box 1992
Bandon, OR 97411
Phone: 541-347-9882; Fax: -9883
E-mail:4bobreed@msn.com
Website: www.rdrpublishers.com

Editors: Joana McCutcheon, Simmi Zaveris, Cynthia Warger, Harmony Blanchard, Kate Rakini, Jill Benz, and Robyn Hessinger

Front Cover Art: *Christmas Angel* © Alien Cat - Fotolia.com

Cover, Editor, and Interior Designer: Cleone L. Reed

Softcover ISBN 13: 978-1-34759-44-8

eBook ISBN 978-1-944297-68-8

Library of Congress Control Number: 2009940895

Formatted and printed in the United States of America.

Dedication

To everyone
Who chooses to
Live in love
And divine service.

Acknowledgments

I appreciate my parents and children—even when they did not understand me; they supported me to follow my heart.

I am grateful to my teachers and clients for all they have taught me about life and spirituality.

I feel honored to be my students' chosen teacher.

I value all my friends who encourage me to be who I am.

I thank my editors: Joana McCutcheon, Simmi Zaveris, Cynthia Warger, Harmony Blanchard, Kate Rakini, Jill Benz, and Robyn Hessinger.

I am grateful to all the angels for assisting me to live a life of love, adventure, and divine service.

Love and Light, Helene

Contents

Introduction

Commitment to Service

The dew was naturally watering the leaves and the colorful flowers; they seemed to sparkle in the rays of the sun. The cloudless sky was a beautiful shade of light blue. God truly has the most versatile and magnificent palette. My morning walk on the mountain road, one spring morning, was not unusual—except for the thoughts that were broadcasting in my head.

"I have to serve! I must be in service! If my loved ones threaten to disown me for following this path, so be it! With no hesitation, I would release them with love to go their own way, as I must go mine."

At that moment, I made a conscious decision to turn my life over to service. Just as a rose is and can only be a rose, I am and can only be an angel on call. From every cell of my body, service became my reason for being, my intent, and my focus—serving for the sake of serving.

It is true that I was already committed to following my intuition and that I was helping people in many ways. I was also using the word "service'" instead of "work," as the former means that I am coming from love. In fact, I realized that people who were coming from love, no matter what they were doing, were healers in service. For example, I noticed how I felt better after a waitress or waiter served me with a warm smile.

However, focusing my life on lovingly assisting others was another level of commitment, and a deep inner peace and joy filled my heart and soul. There were no recent books, teachers, or workshops preceding this precious life-changing moment—although, all of the above helped me reach that place of clarity and make the decision to surrender to divine service. This was simply the moment it all came together in recognition—a time of awakening another level of consciousness—time that started a path of new adventures, way beyond what my mind could possibly know or conceive.

In 1991, the foothills of the Sierra Mountains in California, USA, were a wonderful place to be inspired. My one bedroom, six-hundred-square-foot hilltop cabin overlooked the beautiful rolling mountains and many shades of green-leaved trees. I created a "bedroom" in the loft at the top of a steep flight of stairs. This arrangement allowed me to have a downstairs office.

The two-block town, a former gold mining area flooded with prospectors in the earlier days, was now a sleepy place with some concrete remains of former storefronts.

I often returned from my walks with rocks filled with crystals. I heard that wherever there are crystals, gold is not far away and vice versa. Maybe that high-energy place had something to do with my leap of consciousness and faith. Was I sent there to uncover my deeper life purpose?

Previously, I had been living and counseling in San Jose, California, the area known as Silicon Valley, which is an hour south of San Francisco. How I ended up in the mountains three hours east is another story, which I will share in this book. Suffice it to say, it was all part of the divine plan.

How I arrived to devote my life to service and how it unfolded in the divine plan will be fun to share with you in this book. My goal is to offer you information to expand your horizons, awaken your courage to be all that you are, and to inspire you to reach your true potential.

I have included important clearing and protection information, helpful articles, and empowering excerpts from books that the angelic beings, which I consider to be God's messengers, have written through me. They have helped me on my spiritual path, and they can also assist you. In the last chapters, you will find their loving channeled messages.

Everything in this book is true, except for names of people, which have been changed to protect their privacy, and some of the places, to honor their sacredness. Enjoy the adventure—I certainly have!

PART I

Walk About with the Angels

1: *Latent Gifts*

I arrived on earth in 1940 to lower-middle-class American parents in Brooklyn, New York, USA. They were good people who lived a normal life, according to society's perspective.

As I was growing up, I never heard the words spirituality, service, or intuition. I was a very good athlete, and I loved playing ball games (softball, handball, etc.) and riding my bicycle like it was a bronco. Angels and fairies were not visible to me. My inside time was taken up by reading joke books, playing board and card games, and listening to the radio. When television was invented, it was added to the list.

I was called a tomboy, and I loved wearing my jeans and cowboy hat and pretending to be a tough westerner. The cowboy movies inspired me to have two cap guns sitting on my hip holsters. I think that I took on this tough outer image in order to survive in my rough neighborhood. Looking back, between that and my intuition, I made it to adulthood.

When I was ten years old I found a purse on a park bench containing a wallet bulging with money. My parents were not at home, so I took it to my neighbor's apartment. She found the person's information and called her. The lady cried as she expressed her gratitude to me. She had just taken the money out of the bank to buy Christmas presents. I was rewarded with $10.00, but the wonderful feeling of being kind and helping another was my real gift. The proverb I had learned in grammar school had really influenced me: "Do unto others as you want others to do unto you. "

Physical Education was my favorite subject. I was an average student and often excelled in subjects when I liked my instructor, but sometimes I performed poorly if I disliked the teacher. Looking back now, I realize how sensitive I was to be so affected by others. I imagine that I needed to feel a caring, positive connection in order to

11

excel. Negative vibrations often shut me down. Can you relate to that?

Years later I was married, and my leadership and athletic abilities led me to a Bachelor and Master's Degree in Health and Physical Education. I taught in a tough high school for three years, and then I took leave to birth and take care of my two children. It was amusing, and also sad, to notice that when I returned to teaching eight years later, some of the staff acknowledged my presence as if I had been there straight through. I could see in their eyes how burned out and unmotivated they were. The security of tenure kept them physically in a job they had left emotionally a long time ago.

Two years later I knew it was time for me to leave. On the first day of school in September, I was already counting the days before summer vacation at the end of June. I loved the teaching, but I was frustrated by the large amount of paper work and the overcrowded classes (sometimes as many as 100 to 150 students in a gym class!). I was discouraged by the students' drug and alcohol problems, and their violence with each other and the teachers. I did not appreciate their resistance to learning and the need to discipline them. I felt helpless and angry when I noticed teachers taking their frustrations out on their captive audiences—their students.

I realized that the highlight of my day was when the teenagers came to me with their personal problems. Somehow, I just knew how to help them feel better. I guess it also helped that I cared about them and they knew it.

My marriage had some up times but was mostly downright miserable. Like many women, I blamed my husband for everything. However, I realized much later that we were both very insecure and had poor communication skills—love is not enough! We did the best we could with the information that we had at the time.

Notice my normal or average upbringing and early adult years with no clue as to how my path would be so different from the norm. The only small sign I recall is my dad sometimes saying that I was wise. To me, knowledge is composed of what we learn with our minds (left brain) and wisdom is information from our spirit (right brain). Somehow, I was unconsciously tapping into my internal wisdom.

I guess it all began on my thirtieth birthday. I woke up and said to myself, "Helene, you are not going to spend the next thirty years like the last thirty." It was then that I ventured off into therapy and began to change my life.

Three years later, my husband and I legally and emotionally let go of each other. Of course I felt sad and disappointed, as I had expected to be married forever. However, the overriding feeling was joy and excitement. Feeling free to be me was exhilarating! My higher self-esteem gave me the foundation and the courage to move on in my life.

My ex-husband had remarried and his wife was pregnant. One clear day, while he was walking his dog, a cab driver drove onto the sidewalk and killed them both. It was a freak accident, or was it? Later his family hinted that he was going to kidnap our two young daughters and move to another state. It is interesting that when we were married, he always wanted to visit graveyards. He even once tried to convince me to agree to move into an apartment next to a cemetery.

Ironically, I had supported him through school for ten out of the twelve years we were married. With the insurance money I received, I was able to leave New York State and return to school to study for another Master's Degree.

2: *Move to California*

The following summer, I enrolled my two daughters in a wonderful camp and traveled around the United States to find where I wanted to live and study. When I arrived in San Jose, California, things began to feel right. I quickly made friends who helped me learn about the city.

The University of Santa Clara felt like a school I could relate to, and I started to look for housing. I found an apartment complex that looked promising. When I inquired about any vacancies, the manager said that there was a waiting list and added my name. I was very surprised to receive a phone call the following day informing me that an apartment was available.

I felt excited, but also anxious. It was time to make the big decision. I asked myself what I wanted to do and I heard, "Move to California." Another part of me said, "But I am afraid." The first inner voice said, "So what if you are afraid—do it anyway!" As I reflect on my life, I realize that these encouraging words could be the title of my autobiography.

When I flew back to Brooklyn, New York, and my daughters returned from camp, we packed up and left for our new home three thousand miles away. My parents were sad to see us go, but they accepted my decision. My seven and ten-year-old daughters did not want to leave, but I knew I could offer them a better life in California. I left all my friends and family and a teaching job with tenure because it felt right—because I had the courage to do what I truly wanted to do, which was to follow my heart, even though it was scary.

For some reason, I never felt at home in Brooklyn, even though it was my birthplace. California was a different story. I felt like I was coming home. I loved the weather and the beauty. I loved that the girls could be outside most of the year and have plenty of safe places to play. In 1976, when America was celebrating two hundred years of independence, I was celebrating mine!

I had no idea, however, that my whole life path would change so dramatically. I enrolled in the Santa Clara University counseling program. I also discovered many people in the community who were interested in personal and spiritual growth and healing. Then the spiritual teachers started showing up. I was ready, and I embraced all the wonderful resources. I discovered that I was spiritual and extremely intuitive. I realized that I could see things with my third eye, sense things in my gut, and hear things with my inner ear. Sometimes I even had telepathic knowing.

For many years I had stopped using the word God because I could not relate to what the religions were teaching. It was only after I heard a minister speak at a New Thought Church service that I would again express the higher power word. The all-good, all-knowing, and unconditionally loving God he was talking about was one that resonated with me. I loved connecting with like-minded people, and I learned so much about positive, new thought (although it is really not new).

I also learned that we all have guardian angels that are always looking out for our well-being. However, we have to be willing to listen and act on their guidance. We have free, twenty-four-hour "angel protection," seven days a week and all year long—including holidays. I call it tuning into "GOD radio," produced by the "Company of Heaven." The "Angel Insurance" is priceless!

Another way I understand this phenomenon is that we are here to live from our fifth dimensional, spiritual consciousness in this third dimensional (personality) reality—or live vertically instead of horizontally. This means that when something happens here on earth (horizontal) that is frightening, it serves us to go up (vertical) to receive clarity and guidance.

For example, when I heard about a tragedy on earth and I felt upset, I immediately went up to question my spirit (or angels) through my intuition. "Why did this happen? What can I do to help?" The answers were comforting and helpful. I was then able to move out of my fears and into my love space to make a positive difference.

I realized that stress is basically negative thinking. I decided that it was important for my health and well-being to overcome my fears and to feel love, no matter what happened to others or me. I understood that I am here to make a difference and for my soul growth—to live from unconditional love rather than fear. People who were channeling beings from the light were coming from all over to give presentations in my area. I was impressed with the loving wisdom that came through them and resonated with my heart. I somehow knew to be discerning and to trust only the information that felt true in my heart, even if it sounded very logical and convincing.

To help my teenage daughter receive clarity as to what path to follow, I started to practice channeling. That was another life-altering experience. At this point in my life, I knew that angels and guides were assisting me. However, when I felt a guide in my body talk through me in a different speech pattern, I KNEW they were there. The experience accelerated my trust and faith, and I decided to share the gift with many others. Being a former teacher, I had the ability to pass on whatever I learned. It was a joyful experience to assist many people to connect with their guides and angels. (Note the channeling chapter in Part II).

With courage and conviction, I kept practicing channeling and became really good at surrendering to my higher self and allowing the guides and angels to talk through me. I felt honored and touched when I channeled different beings from the light, including: Archangel Michael, Mother Mary, St. Germain, Isis, and Sananda (the Spirit of Jesus). I invited any beings of the light to channel through me, and they kept coming.

Counseling and lecturing seemed to be my natural ability and I was a very successful Marriage and Family Therapist and speaker. With the goal of sharing what I had learned with more people, I also started writing articles and recording tapes. I could not accommodate all the clients who requested my services, so I founded and directed a non-profit institute where I trained and supervised interns. All that I was doing, plus the normal time and energy necessary for my personal life, caused me to burn out. My grown-up daughters had left home, and I intuitively knew I had to leave the now bustling city to recuperate. However, I had no clue where to go.

One day I received a phone call from Linda, a friend of a friend who knew about my work. She and her husband had just bought a house in the foothills of the Sierra Mountains and they wanted to set up a retreat center. Linda asked me if I would be interested in offering workshops. I was very open to the idea and said, "I know I am also supposed to move. Tell me about the area." Linda described the beautiful country and offered to take me there the following weekend.

The majestic green rolling hills and mountains were very healing to behold. I felt drawn to the sparsely populated area. In my meditation, I had visualized a cabin next to a large pine tree. Motivated to relocate there, I returned the next weekend and started looking for a place to live. When I informed people that I was looking for a cabin, they told me that they were difficult to come by. I did not let them influence me because I trusted my intuitive message.

The Sunday newspaper listed an apartment available in an unfamiliar town. Still exploring the area and wanting to check out all my options, I called the realtor and she gave me directions. As we were walking towards the vacant unit, I said, "I am really looking for a cabin." The surprised realtor answered, "I just signed an agreement with a lady who owns a cabin up the hill. Do you want to see it?" I smiled as I replied, "Yes."

The cabin was small but darling. As I explored each room, ideas of where to put my furniture were coming quickly. There was a beautiful view and a loft. It was very quiet with no other houses close by. Sure enough, there was a beautiful large pine tree in the backyard. I knew I had found my new home.

The realtor and I returned to town and I filled out a rental application. That was probably the fastest she had ever rented a property. I felt overwhelmed with gratitude—the angels had helped me find my healing cabin.

I loved living there and I was very productive. I believe another guide came to me, because the style of my writing improved tremendously, although I did not attend a class or read a book on the subject. It was an awesome place to be inspired. Many posters, cards, books, booklets, tapes, and articles were pouring out of me as fast as I could move my fingers on the keyboard. My first poster,

AS I GROW, was published and sold internationally. Twelve more posters and five cards followed that.

Some of my clients called me, and I discovered that the phone sessions were very effective. I was so pleased that I could serve the world from my little cabin in the mountains. I also offered channeling classes and other workshops. That helped me meet other spiritual people and healers, and some of us set up a healing retreat.

After living in the beautiful, serene mountains for three years, I thought I would be there forever. However, the angelic beings had another plan. To my surprise, one day in August 1992, I was guided to move in April 1993 to Sedona, Arizona. After I overcame the shock, I inquired, "Why?" I intuitively heard there were people there who needed my healing services and others who would assist me.

Meanwhile, I had planned a trip to Hawaii to visit a friend who had just moved there. She wanted me to come in September, but I intuitively heard that I was to go in August. I had fun taking many pictures in beautiful Kauai. Fortunately I had listened to my guidance, as there was a major hurricane in September that destroyed most of the beautiful places I had photographed.

One morning in February, I felt excited when I intuitively heard that I was to purchase tickets to fly to Arizona to find my place in Sedona. The travel agent commented how I had just made the fourteen-day discounted fare.

I had attended a workshop in Sedona about nine years earlier. At the time, probably why I did not feel excited was because I was recovering from a painful relationship break-up, and that was connected with the area. This visit was different. I had tears of joy and my heart felt open.

My intuition guided me to the New Age Center where I shared with the staff that I was looking for a place to stay. A man suggested that I call a lady who was leaving for two weeks and wanted to rent her condo. The accommodation was perfect and very reasonable.

I asked my angels, "Now, how do I find my new home?" The angelic beings replied, "Dearest one, buy a newspaper tomorrow morning. You will find a place to call listed under the Rooms to Rent Ads. That will not be the appropriate place, but the person whom you speak to will tell you the right one to call. You will be living on Lower Red Rock Loop Road."

The next morning, following my guidance with great optimism and curiosity, I picked up the paper and looked through the ads. There was one that seemed attractive because it described country living and views. When I called, a woman named Penny answered the phone and told me that she was on Lower Red Rock Loop Road. I felt excited and I knew that I was on the right track. Then Penny proceeded to describe the room for rent and told me that three adults and two children also lived in the house. I replied, "I don't think that the room will work for me because I am an author and I need a quiet space." Penny responded, "Okay. Then call my neighbor John," and she gave me his address and phone number.

When I tried to call John, I discovered that I had the wrong number. My intuition told me to drive out to the house. When I arrived, I knocked on the door and I heard someone welcome me in.

I introduced myself to the man sitting at the kitchen table and explained why I was there. John, a slim man in his late forties, nodded his head up and down, continued to enjoy his lunch, and pointed to the available master bedroom and den behind him. I walked through the living room and den and entered the bedroom. It was a nice size and had a large window facing the green lawn, trees, and shrubs. I then noticed another door and discovered a very large, two sink bathroom with a tub. I was thrilled, as I hadn't had a bathtub for over three years. Everything was carpeted and nicely furnished. It felt good, quiet, and comfortable. I thought, "I could live here. I have possibly found my sanctuary."

I returned to the kitchen and told John that the space could work for me, but I wouldn't be moving until April (and this was the middle of February). John quickly replied, "I can't hold it for you."

Knowing that I was totally taken care of and guided, I calmly replied, "I understand." Then I placed one of my brochures, which listed my inspirational and self-help books, tapes, cards, and posters, on the kitchen table next to him and said, "I'll call you in March to find out if the rooms are still vacant." I was thinking, "If it's supposed to be my place, it will be available."

I thanked John and walked out of the house. As I was opening the car door, I heard someone calling my name. Sure enough, John was walking towards me with my brochure in his hand. He said, "You're a very interesting person. Would you meet me at the Chinese restaurant in town for dinner tonight at 6 p.m.? We can talk more about renting the room."

Confident that this was perfect, I smiled and replied, "Sure." The restaurant was very nicely decorated and it had a big aquarium with very large colorful fish gracefully swimming around. I was pleased to find out that there was no MSG in the food. That added chemical caused me headaches.

After we got to know each other better, John began telling me about the rental agreement and the details of moving in. Then he suggested that I stay over one night to try it out to make sure that I really liked it. I found that to be very amusing. I had tried out many things, tried on many clothes, but never a room. This was great!

John then told me that he slept in the studio across the driveway and no one else was presently living in the three bedroom house. Feeling safe and guided, I agreed that it was a good idea to sleep there.

The next morning, I walked out of the den and found John sitting on the couch in the living room waiting for me. I could tell that he was anxious to know my answer. He smiled and, almost afraid to ask, said, "Well, how was it?" His face relaxed when I replied, "Great! I like it." John's smile expanded as he said, "I feel like an angel has come into my life." I felt touched.

I gave my new landlord the first month's rent, signed an agreement, and off I went to enjoy the rest of my time in Sedona. I spent many wonderful days hiking on the beautiful red rocks and meeting more like- minded people.

On the flight back home I was feeling quite content and pleased that the mission was successful. I thanked the angelic guides for keeping their agreement of making everything easy for me. I also laughed when I realized why they had told me three months before that I was to give all my furniture away. My new home in Sedona was totally furnished; another confirmation of my clear and accurate inner guidance.

On the morning of April 3rd, my friend David and I started our journey to Arizona in a rental moving truck. I was in the passenger seat enjoying the scenery and feeling very supported. My friends Bill and Heather were following us in their blue station wagon. I felt very excited. Finally, I was on my way! "Sedona, here I come!"

It was a fourteen-hour trip from Sacramento so David and I had plenty of time to talk. He was still wondering why I would want to live in a desert. I couldn't convince him that there were green trees, grass, and mountains. About two hours before we reached our halfway mark, we began to hear some unusual noises under the right fender. Concerned, we pulled into the next gas station, and David jumped out to see what was causing it.

What a treat to drive with a dear friend who is also a mechanic. David is also extremely intuitive. He could diagnosis a car problem over a telephone. I had total trust in his abilities and professional opinions. I felt relieved when David reassured me that we could make it to the town we were heading for and have it fixed there.

A few hours later we arrived in a small city and checked into a motel. I immediately called the emergency number of the moving van company, and I was told that the appropriate local people would contact me. I was impressed how quickly they called and showed up in our parking lot. After they inspected the truck, they told us what had to be fixed. Concerned, we told them that we were planning to head out early the next morning and didn't want to be delayed. The mechanics agreed to take the truck to their repair station and return it within an hour.

Sure enough, at 9 p.m. our repaired truck was returned to us and all was well. I smiled at the perfection of it all—we didn't have to lose any time. We had ended up in a town in the middle of the desert that had twenty-four-hour truck services, even on a Saturday night.

Happy with anticipation, we awoke bright and early the next morning and continued the journey to my new home. Six hours later, we arrived in Flagstaff, a town about thirty miles north of Sedona. David was feeling tired and he asked me to drive the last stretch. I was nervous at the wheel because the beautiful Oak Creek Canyon mountain road was narrow and winding. We were descending from 7,500 feet to an elevation of 4,550 feet. I asked my guides for assistance, and I visualized the white light around us to increase the protection. Then I took a few deep breaths, relaxed more into my seat, imagined us safely arriving at my new home, and trusted that I could do it.

As soon as we were in view of the welcoming Sedona red rocks, David said, "Oh, my God. This is incredible!" I couldn't resist saying, "I told you so, but I understand that this is something you have to see to believe." From that moment on, David acted like a typical tourist. He took out his camera and was constantly shooting pictures of the awesome scenery.

This time when I first saw the familiar red rocks I didn't cry. However, I felt a deep sense of inner peace and joy. At home at last! When we arrived at my new residence, John welcomed us with open arms. After a few minutes of rest and refreshments, Bill and David started unloading my personal and business things. I was so grateful for their support, and they were glad to be able to help me. Two hours later, my new neighbor Kate arrived from San Diego with her packed car and moved into the attached studio apartment adjacent to the house.

My friends and I went to dinner at a Thai restaurant. To our surprise, John was sitting at the next table with a couple that was moving into the middle two bedrooms. Just as the angelic beings had said eight months before, I had to wait until April because the people I was supposed to be with weren't there yet. Never in my life had I rented part of a house and lived with anyone except my husband and children. I asked the angelic beings, "Why now?" They replied, "You have been isolated enough. You now need to be with people to help you heal and grow."

That made sense to me, and I was grateful for the opportunity. It sure felt like a stretch, but I had confidence that I could do it—especially since I could always retreat into my bedroom and be insulated from any noise. I was thankful that the angelic beings had set me up in a safe, comfortable home. The view from the porch was of Cathedral Rock, an incredible natural sculpture of red rocks. I felt warmth in my heart as I gazed at its magnificent beauty. No wonder—later some friends told me that it was known for its feminine heart energy. Just as the angelic beings had told me, I had the opportunity to serve many people in Sedona, and I also had wonderful healings. I loved the beautiful area, and I felt so grateful for the opportunity to call it my home. When tourists stopped me for directions on the country road, they often expressed how lucky I was to live there. I replied, "I was a good girl and this is my reward." I truly was a loyal servant of the light, and the angelic beings take care of and reward their devoted human teammates.

3: *Sedona Spiritual Adventures*

The loving angelic beings were with me on a daily basis, and they guided me on many fun and exciting spiritual adventures. One morning I heard, "Go to the canyon off Dry Creek Road." The dirt road was like a washboard. Even though I was driving slowly, clouds of dust formed behind me. I pulled into the parking area and prepared myself for the trust walk by taking two deep breaths and visualizing myself returning to the car feeling wonderful. I grabbed my hiking stick, water bottle, sunhat, and backpack. I was ready!

Then I spoke the prayer that I use before going out on the land. With my eyes closed, I took a few deep breaths and set my intent. I said, "I ask permission to enter this land in love, peace, and gratitude." When I intuitively heard that I was welcomed, I continued, "I request that the animal and plant Devas protect me, and I thank you for your love and support. And so it is!"

Confident that I was safe, I tuned-in and began to listen to the angelic beings' directions. I heard, "All is well, dear one, go straight." After about five minutes, I was guided to turn to the left and a short distance later to the right. Not wanting to disturb any of the natural habitats that I appreciated and respected, I walked carefully and with great reverence.

After about twenty minutes of following my intuitive voice, my eyes moved to the right and I noticed something that looked very interesting. I stopped, bent down, and realized that it was a stick that looked like a snake, but fortunately wasn't. I stood up and began to walk forward again when I heard, "Dear one, you have arrived at the destination. Please sit here."

A trusting soul, I sat down and found myself next to the snake-like stick. "Pick up the stick and hold it in your hands. It is a gift for you," said the angelic beings in their usual loving, gentle voice. As I lifted the unusual object in my hands, I felt an incredible amount of energy radiating from it. Then they requested that I close my eyes and turn inward.

My body felt very warm and tingly. I was aware that the angelic beings were sending energy through me in the form of white light. It felt very nurturing and healing. I knew that they were once again helping me to recover from burnout, and to raise my vibration so that I could be clearer and maintain a state of love. Tears of joy and gratitude were flowing down my cheeks as I felt my heart open to take in this high dosage of love.

After this wonderful healing experience, the angelic beings asked me to take the snake-like stick home and guided me back to my car. As I was driving home, I glanced at the small, thin branch sitting next to me. I smiled as I realized that I had never felt such reverence for a stick as I did for this one. I understood that the wooden snake-shaped object was obviously touched by my angelic guides, and it was a conduit of their high vibration energy.

I was guided to many more enjoyable and exhilarating spiritual hikes with other people and by myself. When I told my friends about the incredible adventures, they looked skeptical. However, after they joined me and also had divine experiences, they were hooked. They were touched by the spiritual encounters and amazed by the way we were always guided straight back to the car, even though we often felt lost. When I called my friends and asked, "Do you want to join me on another angelic adventure?" they responded with great enthusiasm, "Just tell me when and where to meet you."

One day my friend Lynne and I were guided to one of the national forest lands. As usual, the angelic beings directed us when to go straight or turn. We ended up in a very beautiful part of the red rocks where the view was awesome. The angelic beings asked us to sit down and meditate. We found comfortable places, closed our eyes, and listened within. After about twenty minutes, Lynne and I opened our eyes and talked about our experiences. We both heard very loving, comforting words, and we shared a common feeling of delicious inner peace.

Then I heard, "Dear ones, please touch the dead-looking tree in front of you." Lynne and I walked the few feet to the leafless tree and placed our hands on one of the branches. To our surprise, we instantly felt a tremendous amount of energy radiating into our hands. The angelic beings continued, "Dear ones, this tree is obviously dead and not receiving energy from the earth. The intense energy you feel is coming from us." My friend and I looked at each other and laughed. This was more physical proof that they were there, or maybe they were somewhere else in the galaxy. The angelic beings were definitely communicating with us and sending us cosmic energy. What fun!

I was pleased to notice how extremely compassionate and understanding the angelic beings were with our human need for confirmation of these extraordinary events. On another hike, three of my friends and I were guided to approach a wall of rocks with the same reverence we would have for a holy temple. As we leaned our backs against the red rocks and closed our eyes, we felt loving energy, heard encouraging words, and visualized colorful images. We all walked away feeling like something incredibly special had happened—something wonderful had touched us deeply. We felt light and knew that we had received a healing—we felt very humble and grateful.

There were times when I thought that I might be crazy. I wondered what the true reality was. One day I said out loud, "Will the real reality please show up?" Guess what? I saw both worlds. I began to accept my multidimensional citizenship. It sure made life very interesting and great fun!

On another adventure with two friends, Kim and Pat, we were guided to a national forest that had many washes—places where water used to flow. As we were hiking in, Kim came across some heart-shaped rocks. She picked up a small one and then a little bigger one. They were precious and were actually shaped like the hearts on our Valentine cards. Kim asked the rocks if she could take them home. The small one said "Yes," and the bigger one said "No." Kim placed the smaller heart-shaped rock into her pocket and put the larger one back where she had found it. We feel that it is most important to honor Mother Earth and all the plants, animals, rocks, and minerals. We do not assume that it is okay to take something home, so we always first ask for permission.

Continuing along, we were guided to turn right, and we came upon an area where there were many different pathways to a magnificent wash. The three of us felt like we were walking in the veins and arteries of Mother Earth. A little further down, we came across some large rocks, and the angelic beings asked us to sit there and meditate. We separated a little to give each other space, sat down, and closed our eyes.

After about twenty minutes, we opened our eyes and began to share our experiences. Kim expressed that she was suddenly aware of an incredible silence and absolute stillness. She heard no birds, wind, or insects, and that stillness actually brought Kim out of her meditation because it was so different from how it was before. She felt total peace.

I had a very different experience. I had been processing some issues. A previous conversation with a friend didn't feel good, and I was asking the angelic beings to help me release my upset. I said, "Show me the wisdom and the meaning to all of this so that I can grow and let it go, as I know it is my issue. I choose to feel good and peaceful."

My spiritual part knew that the upset is never about the other person. It is always about how I perceive what the other person is saying and what my mind decides it means about me. Two of my favorite sayings are, "What people say or do is a reflection of them and not of you," and, "No matter what people say or do, you are okay!"

However, even though I know the above truths, my personality had "hooked in," and I felt angry with my friend and scared that I was not okay. With the help of my angelic friends, I was able to release the illusion. I saw my emotional pain leave my body in the form of a dark color. Then white light flowed into me to replace the void and help me cleanse. I felt much better after this short but very sweet healing meditation.

After Pat also shared how peaceful she felt, we were guided to climb up a hill. To our surprise, we found ourselves standing at the edge of a very large, beautiful meadow. I had hiked in this forest a few times before, but for some reason I had never walked into this area. We smiled, as we were pleased with the peaceful feeling and the breathtaking view. I then heard to go to the right. It seemed as though we were making a complete circle.

27

At one point we came across a very special tree. There were no other trees around it. When we touched its bark we felt male energy. It was a very balanced masculine energy, as it had strength, but it also had softness to it, which is the feminine energy. As we talked to the tree, we heard that it was very grateful that it was there, and it was joyfully watching over the meadow. Then the three of us were aware of feeling very intense but wonderful energy under our feet. When we asked the tree what was creating the energy under us, it said, "It is crystal energy. There are crystals under the ground." No wonder it felt so wonderful!

The angelic beings had told me, as we were climbing that last hill to come up to the meadow, that there was something very special for us when we arrived there. I had no idea what it was. We enjoyed the very peaceful meadow and the crystals under the ground. However, the wonderful tree was our special treat.

As I was driving home, I kept seeing the image of the tree in the middle of the meadow and I knew that it had some significance for me. It stayed with me until I explored the meaning of the image when I was comfortable in my bed. The tree reflected something in my personal life—something that I was identifying with. I realized that I was getting ready to go out in the world again as a leader and as a teacher to share what I had learned. I noticed that even though I was excited about fulfilling my mission, I also had some fears. I heard myself thinking, "It's lonely at the top." I was afraid that when I did succeed, I would be alone.

The image of that one tree standing alone in the meadow doing its service naturally became a symbol of strength for me. It reminded me that I would be fine and able to serve in joy, peace, and harmony. I was very grateful for the experience and the image.

In another awesome experience, one hot summer day five of my friends and I were guided to journey up to another sacred place of the angelic beings. Two years ago they had taken me to one of their special places on top of a large flat rock. I had already taken numerous groups up there, and each time everyone reported something wonderful happening to them. I was once again excited to share this profound spiritual experience with my friends, Paul, Amber, Jerry, Lois, and Caren.

Only Amber had been up there with me before. The group had decided to meet at 6 p.m. because it would hopefully be cooler at that time. About 5:20 p.m. the sky darkened and, typical of this monsoon season, it started to rain. Concerned about the weather, Amber and I kept checking in with our guides, the "cosmic weather people," as to whether or not to continue as planned. It didn't seem logical, but we were reassured that all was well. However, I followed my guidance to put my poncho into my backpack.

Trusting in their "green light," the group met on schedule and drove up the dirt mountain road. Three miles later we arrived at the place to park and were greeted by an amazing, full rainbow. When we got out of the car to marvel about it, we realized that we were standing right in the middle of the half circle of colorful lights. We felt excited and extremely blessed as we formed a circle and expressed our intent and gratitude and asked for protection.

Because the rocks were wet from the rain, we teamed up and held hands to help each other stay on our feet and proceeded very carefully up the trail. I took the lead to guide my dear open-minded friends. Half way up I heard the words, turn around. I smiled as I saw the double rainbow lighting up the sky. What a sight! I laughed, because when I had first seen the single rainbow, the angelic beings had told me, "There will be a double," and there it was.

Just before we approached the sacred area, I shared with the group that when I had previously taken a ten-year-old girl up here, she told us to stop and wait while she opened the "door." This delightful, angelic, clairvoyant child saw the sacred temple.

Finally, we climbed the last rock and were standing about ten feet away from our destination. I asked everyone to stand in a line, shoulder to shoulder. With our hands in prayer position we asked for permission to enter. When we telepathically received a joyful welcome, quietly, and with great reverence, we approached the small circle of sand in the midst of a very large flat rock. As we turned around, we noticed that we were still standing in the center of the rainbows and they seemed to be getting closer to us. This did not seem logical because we were walking away from the colorful demonstration of love and light. We all felt honored and touched.

Around this ethereal spiritual circle were a few rocks that we were able to use for seats. Once we were all comfortable, we closed our eyes and began our meditation. At one point I opened my eyes and was aware of the sound of rain drops hitting my poncho, which was very wet by now. However, when I looked at the other five people, I couldn't see any signs of water on their T-shirts. They all seemed so peaceful in their meditation.

Lois suddenly started to cry as she said, "I know my next step. I know what I'm to do. It's time for me to finish writing my children's stories. I started my book twenty years ago. Thank you. Thank you. Thank you!"

Lois had shared earlier that she and her husband Jerry were selling their restaurant business. They each had a calling deep inside of them— something they wanted to express was ready to burst out. Jerry had identified his mission of conducting workshops and lectures. Up until that moment, Lois had no clue of what was next for her.

When we all came back to consciousness, Lois smiled, looked into my eyes, and expressed her deep gratitude to me for bringing her to this special ethereal place. Jerry did the same. Although he was quiet all the time, obviously a lot had happened for him, too.

Six weeks after our group encounter of the most delightful kind, I met Lois at the health food store. She smiled and said, "I usually go down the other aisle to get to the deli, but I had an intuitive message to walk this way today. I have been meaning to call you to tell you about my miraculous healing at the sacred site. When we were sitting in the circle and meditating, I was feeling a chill, but I wasn't cold. It was my body's reaction to the energy that was coming through me.

"A week later, I became very sick. After a few days I realized that I felt terrible only after I took my pills for my asthma. I intuitively heard, 'Dear one, you do not need these pills anymore. They are making you ill.' It took all of my courage to flush the few that I had down the toilet. After all, these pills have been a crutch for me for over twenty-five years. Almost immediately I started to feel fine

"By the end of the week, I felt better than ever. My husband Jerry could not believe the difference in my color and energy. Truthfully, neither could I. My logical mind still wanted to be checked out by a medical doctor. To my surprise, my doctor said, 'I would advise you to keep breathing in white light.' When I checked in intuitively to see if I still needed my aspirator, I heard, 'Keep that with you now but you won't need it much longer.' I can't tell you how grateful I am to you and the angelic beings. Thank you! I will surely never forget our spiritual hike."

Needless to say, I was very happy to hear about Lois's amazing progress. I was also very grateful to be the catalyst for the divine healing. All I was doing was having the courage to follow my intuition without hesitation.

One afternoon I was suddenly guided to go to my mailbox on the road. Since most of my letters went to my post office box in town, I did not feel the need to go to the other one very often. Therefore, I hesitated to act on my message. However, I immediately heard it again. Being an obedient angel on call, I put on my sun hat and walked down the road to the mailbox. Just as I was about to approach it, a navy blue vehicle stopped near me. Two ladies were sitting in the car and they asked me for directions. As I proceeded to guide them to where they wanted to go, I heard, "Tell them what you do." I ignored the comment until I heard it again. When I shared what I offer, the ladies' mouths dropped in surprise. The one in the passenger seat said, "I had just commented to my friend that I wanted to have a reading." I smiled and invited them to turn around and follow me the block down to my home.

The middle-aged woman sat anxiously at the edge of my couch. She told me that she was leaving her computer job and did not know what she wanted to do with her life. I tuned in to the angels and heard that she is a singer. When I told her, "You are a singer," she burst into tears. It was a long-lost love of hers, and I had triggered her memory of what makes her heart feel truly alive. Then I answered some of her questions about her sons. With a big smile on her face, she invited me to come to her home in Detroit to offer readings for her family members and friends. I felt touched and grateful! What an honor it was to assist people back to their hearts!

4: *Angels on Vacation*

The angelic beings were with me all the time—even on vacations. They always seemed to take the opportunity to serve others and me, wherever I went. My friend Sheryl and I had decided to take a trip up to Vancouver. To our surprise, we were guided not to rent a car in Canada and to trust that we would be taken care of at all times. As two intuitive, brave souls, we had the courage to have faith even though we had lots of heavy luggage for our two-week camping trip.

When we were on the plane towards our first destination, I asked the angelic beings how we were going to get to the ferry. "Dear one, a man with a black car will come and take you," was their answer. My first reaction was, "You have to be kidding." I thought that they were joking because they wanted me just to wait and let it happen. Doubts ran through my mind, but I still had faith we would be taken care of.

The airport terminal was noisy and very crowded with passengers coming and going. Sheryl and I made our way to the bus reservation counter and waited our turn. Meanwhile, when we were talking to the tall, young man behind us, we discovered that we were going to the same destination. The clerk informed us that we would never make the ferry on time if we took the bus. She recommended that we chip in for a limousine, which would be even cheaper. The idea sounded very logical and appealing. We signed up for the service and made our way out of the airport. Almost immediately, a man in a black limousine pulled up to take us to our destination. I laughed and apologized to the angelic beings for doubting their words.

Soon after, the angelic beings came to our rescue once again. Sheryl and I had a lot of difficulty bringing our luggage up the small elevator on the ferry. After a few trips and some help from other passengers, we made it to the main level feeling exhausted. Just then a man walked by in a uniform. I said, "Excuse me. Do you know where we can store our luggage?" The tall, dark-haired employee replied, "Sure, I'll take it and you can just pick it up at the port after you get off the ferry." It turned out that the man standing in front of us on this very large, busy ferry was the one responsible for people's luggage. Thank you angelic beings!

The boat ride was delightful. I always love being on the water; it feels so soothing. It was a real treat to be temporarily unburdened of all our gear. We purchased some food and sat in a big, comfortable booth. I closed my eyes and asked the angelic beings, "Who will transport us from this ferry to the next one?" The answer was, "Dear one, you will be taking a cab." When I questioned why we couldn't just ask for a lift they responded, "The person who will transport you needs your services."

I thought I was on vacation, but I guess an angel on call performs her divine service all the time. I opened up to the experience but my mind still thought that it was logical to try to find a lift. However, the woman I approached, who came to pick up her friends at the port, did not have enough room for us. Meanwhile, Sheryl was on the telephone calling for a cab.

About ten minutes later I noticed that no one was around. Fortunately, our ride finally showed up. The cab driver somehow managed to get us and all of our baggage in his car with some creative packing. When we were on our way, the slim, gray-haired man in his fifties asked us where we were from. One thing led to another, and I started to share spiritual concepts with him. He looked at me and said, "My whole family is into those things. I am having a difficult time staying sober. Thank you! Meeting you is a real gift; you made my day. I feel inspired to listen more to what they are saying and doing." I smiled and thought, "Just an angel in service."

5: *Surprise Relocation*

About six months after I had moved into my small space in Sedona, all the roommates moved away and I rented the entire house for many years. Every time I thought of buying my own place, I heard that I was moving. However, it seemed like it was internal and not "out there." Once again, I was convinced that this would be my permanent home. Needless to say, I was shocked when I received the intuitive message that I was being sent to a new destination. After ten years, the angelic beings were guiding me to relocate to Carmel Valley, California. When I asked why, I heard that I was complete in Sedona and I would have a lot more opportunities to serve many more people in California. No specific time was given to me.

I mentioned my message to Sandy, my friend and landlord. She smiled and shared with me that she was intuitively feeling that it was time for her to move out of the studio and into the home I was renting. But she knew that it would be divine timing—she reassured me that she would not pressure me to leave. When I asked Sandy about the furniture that she had acquired when she purchased the property from John four years earlier, she told me that I could take what I needed. That was a relief, because I did not have any furniture of my own. The angelic beings kept proving to me that I could always trust them to provide me somehow with what I needed.

I was grateful that the angelic beings gave me time for my personality to adjust to the move—to leave my majestic surroundings, my students, and my dear friends. About two months later, I received an inner message to start getting rid of things. Then the guidance was to start packing. By the end of March 2004, I was to pack everything I could that I was not using.

I was expecting to move at the beginning of April but heard nothing more. Meanwhile, my friends offered to fly me to Carmel for the weekend to look for a place. I was very grateful, but intuitively received a message not to go. That was not logical, but it was typical of the angel trust walk.

One morning I heard, "Your car cannot go to California. Call the Dodge dealer for your blue Dodge Caravan." The sales person said he had a few Caravans and I told him I would be there on Friday.

On Thursday I had an appointment with my chiropractor, Jason, and I mentioned what was happening with the car. His eyes opened wide and he asked me what I was asking for my car. When I told him, he replied, "This morning I told the angels I had that exact amount of money for another car." We hopped into my minivan and he drove it straight to his mechanic.

On Friday I called Jason to find out if he definitely wanted my car. He did. While I was on the phone with him, the sales person called and said, "I was off yesterday and I just walked the lot. I have your car." I knew he was right. Sure enough, I was shown an aquamarine 2002 Dodge Grand Caravan Sport on sale for $4,000 below the standard price.

Now that I had my new vehicle, I waited for the next message. Two weeks later, my inner voice said, "Call a mover from the yellow pages." I was guided whom to call and two men came to give me an estimate. One told me $3,000. The other said I could save money if I rented a truck and trailer for my car, and he would take care of the rest. He also informed me that I could negotiate a lower price, and that I needed a bigger truck than I had thought. He would take me, but wanted to leave at 3 a.m. and drive straight through.

It sounded good, but I dreaded the fifteen-hour drive with a stranger to whom I did not relate. I wanted to take my time and be with a like-minded person. The next morning I called my friend Stan, who had moved back to Los Angeles, California. I asked him if he would come and help me move. I almost fell off my chair when he said, "Yes." I always say, "If you ask for what you want, you may get it."

Stan arrived in Sedona the next day. He and two other male friends took two days to load all my things into the twenty-four-foot moving truck. Finally, they attached the car trailer to the back of the truck, and we were off on our journey. Stan was easy to be with, and he drove all three days. We had fun, too. We saw a sign that said, "If you want a sign of God, here it is."

On the third day, we were heading toward a small city. I received a message from my angels to eat Chinese food for lunch. I told Stan that I was being guided to purchase gas, and the attendant would tell us where to eat. Sure enough, we were told about a restaurant a few blocks away. It was fantastic—the best Chinese restaurant buffet! Feeling very grateful, I told Stan, "The angelic beings even know the great places to eat."

We finally reached our destination and pulled into the truck rental parking lot around 3 p.m. To our surprise, the office was closed. Fortunately, there was a mechanic in the lot fixing other trucks. He told us that it would be okay to leave the truck there, and he suggested that we drop a note through the office door mail slot. Stan moved my car off the trailer and we took off. What a joy it was to be in my comfortable car after driving fifteen hours in a noisy, rough-riding diesel truck.

The angelic beings guided me to get a cell phone and drive up to Carmel Valley. It was so beautiful—I saw green mountains, grape vines, farms, a variety of trees, colorful flowers, and many horses. With a big grin on my face, I told Stan, "I can live here!"

The next day we set out to look at places to rent. The few homes we saw were disappointing and expensive. I kept the faith and was told I would find my place the following day.

Stan left early in the morning to fly back to Los Angeles for a conference. I went to see an apartment and almost took it. It was big and beautiful (remodeled), but I was determined not to settle and live in an apartment again with someone over me.

The next morning, I intuitively heard to call my friend Mary in Kentucky. She was very excited to hear from me, because all morning she had been sending me a telepathic message to call her. Mary had recently connected with Susan, a nice realtor who was nearby. I immediately called Susan and discovered she was a few minutes from my hotel. When I arrived at her office, the friendly realtor had already marked off rental places in the paper for me. Her assistant also tried to help me.

After a few more days of searching for my new home, I realized that there was a difference between settling and being realistic. I called back the manager of the apartment I had seen a few days ago and rejected. I knew that if it was mine it would still be available. It was!

The manager gave me the number for the phone company and informed me that it would take a few days to turn it on. However, when I called in the morning, I was told that it would be connected by 5 p.m. I was very grateful because I had scheduled phone sessions on the following day.

I called Susan to tell her the good news and asked her if she knew someone who could move me in. The helpful realtor connected me with a lady who agreed to meet me at the truck after work with her husband and fifteen-year-old son who was 6'5" tall.

I arrived at the truck rental place at 4 p.m. and discovered that the gate to the parking lot was locked and the office was closed. Somehow I remained calm and trusting, and I went to a gas station to use the rest room. When I returned, I saw the same mechanic Stan and I had met when we first pulled in. He was backing his truck out of the lot. He told me that the temporary attendant had locked him in and he had to break the lock.

I asked him to remove the car-trailer that was still attached to the back of my moving van. He backed his truck up and took care of it. Five minutes later my moving crew showed up. They jumped into the moving van and followed me to my apartment. At 9:30 p.m. they finished unloading all my things and drove the truck back to the rental place for me. I felt tired, but so grateful to be in my new apartment. It seemed like the angels also had a busy day—I am sure that they helped me co-ordinate the successful move.

I loved my new home. Each of the two large bedrooms had bathrooms, regular closets, and walk-in closets. Both sides of the apartment had views of majestic mountains. My living room had a large sliding door that opened up to a former small vintage airport where I could walk, fly a kite, etc. I sometimes saw people riding their horses and practicing jumping. The charming town was a block away. The angels took me to another paradise.

Events quickly started to happen to reveal why I was there. After an appointment with a local chiropractor, the receptionist told me that the next patient was a lady who had a radio show. The door opened and there she was. We set a day for my live interview.

I went to a bookstore nearby and Sally, the owner, agreed to sell my posters. I had lunch in their café and as I was leaving, she called me over to her table. Sally informed me that she had called the coordinator of the Writers Organization and recommended me as a feature speaker. By the time I returned home, there was a message on my voice mail from the coordinator.

Many more cosmic occurrences continued to happen, and I was so grateful and happy. I believe that God and I have teamed up to actualize our divine plan. All I do is stay tuned-in and allow the divine plan to unfold with ease and grace.

Friends have called me courageous. The truth is that walking with the angels makes it fun and easy. When I awaken I think, "I wonder what God has in store for me today."

I did some workshops and one of the attendees said, "I intuitively know you will not be in the area very long and I want to learn as much as possible from you. I feel you were sent here to help my family and me."

I heard those words numerous times, as I served those who were open to my insights, teachings, and counseling.

6: *International Angel on Call*

I was intuitively informed that I would only be in California about two years and then return to a different part of Arizona. However, typical of life and angelic messages, things can change. Well, they did, big time!

After being there fourteen months, I woke up one morning to the words, "Dear one, you are to sell everything and move to Australia." Needless to say, I was totally shocked. Nothing happened to prepare me for this international relocation. I was not thinking of Australia, nor had I recently read or seen anything about the country. I kept asking my angelic guides for confirmation, and the answer was always the same. When I asked my intuitive friends to check in with their guidance, they received the same information—Australia was my next destination.

This was major and scary!!!! This was the first time I was asked to sell everything—even my office stuff. What a leap of faith!

I was thankful that the angelic beings gave me a few months to adjust to the move and to emotionally let go of practically everything—my great apartment, the beautiful area, all my furniture, office equipment, crystals, books, CDs, etc. Of course, I also needed the time to get used to the idea of being far away from my friends, students, two wonderful daughters, and beautiful grandchildren (they were an hour and a half away).

In October I was guided to start getting rid of things. At the end of the month, I was told to give the manager the required thirty-day notice on the apartment. My anxiety level went sky high, and one of my students offered to help me process my fears.

Sitting in my beautiful living room, I asked my guides if I was to give all this up. To assist me they visually showed me living in a beautiful place in Australia. That helped, plus a thought that gave me the courage — I am sixty-four years old and life is an adventure. The angelic beings had taken good care of me all along, and I trusted they would again. They had a plan that would help me with my goal of touching many more people, and I was ready to walk (fly) internationally with them.

It was fun to sell all the furniture that was originally John's, the previous owner of the home I rented in Sedona. When I had moved to Sedona, I was guided to give all my furniture to my daughters. I had good "furniture karma."

All I knew was that I was to go to a southern city called Melbourne and offer something at a university. One of my California students, Cindy, was from that area and had friends who had moved to the Gold Coast, which is up North. When I contacted the couple, Barry and Ellen, they graciously invited me to come and stay in their home. Grateful for their warm welcome, I planned to fly to their haven.

The plane tickets were very expensive, so I asked Cindy to help me out. After an hour, she called to give me the number of a company that offered a ticket for almost half the price. I immediately followed up, but the ticket was not available. However, the salesman told me that if I left the day before, I could save another $500. I smiled as I confirmed the reservation. The angelic beings did it again!

The Australian Gold Coast was beautiful, but I intuitively knew that it was not where I was to settle. However, I had a much needed vacation and enjoyed the area as well as the sights. Barry and Ellen were great hosts, and I loved eating the fresh avocados and mangos that fell from their trees. It was fun to watch the family of four kangaroos also enjoying the delicious fruit. I loved the amazing view from their beautiful home in the country, and I appreciated my big bedroom and private bathroom.

One day I told Ellen that I intuitively knew that I needed to move to Melbourne. Her friend Sarah, who lived in one of the suburbs, welcomed me to her home. After two hot but wonderful weeks in the Gold Coast, I flew to Melbourne. Sarah met me at the airport and took me to her beautiful home. Once again, I had great accommodations. Sarah introduced me to Cathy, a tarot reader she had gone to for readings. Cathy and I both realized that we were meant to connect.

40

The following weekend, she took me to Melbourne for an interesting event. The Spiritualist Church had invited a speaker from England to present a workshop on spirituality. I was excited to go and meet like-minded people.

I realized I needed to be in the city of Melbourne to find out where I belonged and what I was to be doing. I asked a lady who worked for Cathy to drive me there, and I stayed at a hotel. At first it was fun to shop in the market and take the trams to the sights; but the bustling city energy started getting to me, and I knew I had to leave. I had contacted two universities and they were not interested in my services. Obviously, they were not the schools the angelic beings were talking about.

When I had stayed at Sarah's house, I had walked into town and met a naturopath who had owned a health food store. Twice he had told me to go to Daylesford because it was a very healing place. Remembering his words, I asked a lady I had met at the hotel to drive me there.

We arrived in the beautiful two-block town in the afternoon and had lunch in a health food store. That was great for me, since I am very health conscious. I checked into a small two-room condo with a kitchenette and telephone access for a week. Unfortunately, it had some broken doors and other problems, and I did not have a good place to write. Therefore, I was very pleased when they decided to move me next door because the phone was not working.

This two-story, one-bedroom condo was much bigger and nicer. It had a full kitchen, living room, and dining room with a large table to write on. It would have cost much more, but I did not have to pay the difference. I smiled as I thought: once again the angelic beings helped me create what I needed.

The next morning, I decided to walk around the town to see what was available. As I passed by one of the buildings, I noticed a flyer about a female tarot reader. Without hesitation, I walked upstairs and found one of the office doors open. A middle-aged man was sitting behind his desk and working at the computer. I walked in and introduced myself. Dean graciously invited me to sit down. Then I shared my story and my request for information about an inexpensive place to rent. His wife and tarot reader, Angela, joined us, and I briefly shared with her, too. The couple were all smiles and were very welcoming. Since it was lunch time, they took me to the health food store and treated me to a delicious meal.

Dean offered to take me to a meditation group that night; I felt very grateful. I smiled, as things seemed to be flowing rather well. After the meditation, Dean introduced me to some other members of his fellowship, and I repeated my story. I was warmed by their openness and willingness to assist me.

The next day I received a phone call about the availability of an inexpensive accommodation. After a week at the hotel, I needed to move to my new residence on a Sunday, and Dean was unavailable.

The day before, I was in one of the stores in town and struck up a conversation with a young couple visiting the area. A few hours later, I was guided to the health food store for a snack and spotted the couple having tea. We conversed again, and I mentioned that I needed help to move all my luggage to another place. They were happy to assist me. The next day, the big, strong, young male lifted my heavy luggage as if it were paper. I was so grateful!

I enjoyed my new quarters. It consisted of a nicely decorated, large bedroom with a bathroom in a two-story building. I had access to a television, kitchen, and telephone. While I was staying there, I was able to meet many more like-minded individuals. I felt as though I had somehow found one of my spiritual families. Some of them invited me to their homes for dinner.

I often spent one day a week with a sweet, retired lady, Jane. When we met, we felt an instant connection. Both Libras, we seemed to be so much alike and had lots of fun together. Jane took me to another town to buy warm clothes, as the days were getting colder. We also enjoyed eating out, going to the movies, and exchanging healing sessions.

One day Jane shared with me that her angels had told her that something special was going to happen this year, and she felt that it was meeting me. I felt touched.

Jane lived in a beautiful, large three-bedroom home with many possessions I had sold in America and was starting to miss. When I asked her if I could move in, my new friend was glad to have me. Jane offered me one of her large desks and a desk chair and graciously made me feel at home. Needless to say, I felt very grateful to live in a wonderful, quiet, warm, and cozy home with a great view. A charming lake with ducks and swans was a block away. I could stroll around it as well as walk to the town. My cute room turned out to be a wonderful place to write, and I was very productive.

However, I still did not know the main reason why I was brought to Australia. I could have remained in my home in California to write more books, etc.

The mystery was soon to be solved. One of the ladies I met at the meditation group was a member of an organization that wanted to make a difference in the way businesses were conducted. She and others had organized a meeting in the town hall to discuss the community and what improvements could be made. I was intuitively guided to attend.

The large old building was very cold that night in March, and I was wondering why I was there. My inner voice reassured me that I was to stay. After a short group meeting, we were asked to break up into small groups. Four circles of chairs were set up around the room. I was guided to sit in the circle in the right, front corner. Slowly but surely, men and women came to fill the other seats. We all had a chance to share our thoughts on positive changes.

The lady to the left of me seemed to be very nice, and I knew that I was to connect with her. At the break, I turned to Gail and introduced myself. I smiled when I discovered that she was developing an online university. I told her about the self-help on-line program I had written and was about to include on my website. Gail's eyes opened wide as she expressed her interest. We agreed to meet at her home on the weekend.

Here was the university I was guided to connect with. How I found it was pretty amazing. I was definitely guided by the angels. Gail was thrilled to include the valuable information on her university website and make it available to all students. I always knew that I would reach many more people internationally. This was one fantastic way to actualize my goal. What an exciting opportunity, and I had arrived here just when the university was about to get up and running. The angels sure had a plan when they sent me to Australia. I was so happy that I had had the courage to follow my guidance.

Meanwhile, Jane had booked a trip to Western Australia to visit with her children. One day I received the message to fly there also. I had a guest book when I lived in Arizona. Before I left America, I had taken out all the names of those from New Zealand and Australia. My intuition told me to call a couple who came to my home for a reading in Sedona more than eleven years ago. To my surprise, Rosie remembered me and invited me to stay at her home. In fact, she was touched, as her daughter was having a physical problem and the doctors were not able to help her. Rosie's friend had just suggested that she contact a clairvoyant. Then I called. After we agreed for me to come, she burst into the bedroom teary-eyed and told her husband, "I don't believe this!" I was honored and grateful to once again be an angel on call.

I smiled when I noticed my AS I GROW poster and my card, A PROMISE OF LOVE, displayed in their home. They had purchased them when they had visited me in Sedona. How satisfying it is to make a difference in people's lives.

I had to leave Australia soon, because my visa was about to expire. It was a pleasant surprise to intuitively hear that Hawaii was my next destination. So I started having fun networking with people who live on the islands. A friend of mine in Sedona wrote to me about a lady, Sue, who was her roommate before moving to one of the Hawaiian Islands. When I called Sue, she informed me that she was an Australian from the city of Melbourne and often visited Daylesford. She had heard about me in Sedona and was happy to help me in any way that she could. It really is a small world.

My journey was now taking me to beautiful Hawaii. My excitement helped me leave my many loving friends in Daylesford. I knew that I would always be welcomed back. I also trusted that wherever I went, I would create a spiritual family and serve for the highest good of all. I felt a deep inner peace and a great sense of adventure.

By now, I had learned to let go of attachment to things and people, including my dear children and grandchildren. Friends and I may be teary- eyed when I leave, but I knew that we can always stay in touch. Like everyone, I do need to give and receive love. However, there are many people who can fulfill that need. It is up to me to keep my heart open and be as loving as I can be. I love the quote, "True success is not determined by your accomplishments but by how much you have expressed caring and love to others and yourself."

I never know where my next dollar is coming from but I trust that I am on "God's payroll." I always manage to receive what I need to live in a simple, comfortable way. The money I earn through international telephone sessions, book sales, workshops, and lectures pays my bills and feeds me physically. However, the fulfilment I receive for my angelic services feeds my soul and keeps me going. It is such a joy to be who I am, to do what I came here to do, and to trust and have faith in the divine plan.

At my age, most people are retiring. However, that word is not in my vocabulary. Although I have already touched many millions of people, I feel as though I am just getting warmed up.

Before I had left for Australia at the request of the angels, I sold everything except a laptop computer, a portable printer, luggage, and some clothes. I no longer had a physical, permanent home, as the angels move me around the world to serve. Home is where my heart is, and I take it wherever I go.

Everything I do professionally has the intent to assist people to "love themselves to peace," which I believe is the key to health, happiness, success, and world peace. Everything that I do personally is focused on helping me to be healthy and to love others and myself unconditionally.

I am constantly choosing love rather than fear. It is my belief that joy and laughter are signs of God's presence, and I look for the humor in all situations. I am committed to being positive and to maintaining trust and faith no matter what happens. When I leave this earth plane, I will be able to say that I truly lived.

I used to be afraid of the unknown. Now I say the following positive words: "I walk forward into the known in ease, grace, joy, love, and light as my spirit knows it all." I follow my intuition, my inner wisdom, with no hesitation. My commitment is to live the rest of my life in service as an angel on call!

7: *The Journey Continues*

"Welcome home!" was the airport security guard's remark when he reviewed my passport. I felt touched when I realized I was welcomed back to my birth home, America. My ten months in the gorgeous Hawaiian Islands were also a treat. I had the opportunity to live, explore, and serve in the four large islands; Maui, Hawaii, Oahu, and Kauai. I continued to offer my healing services that were very much appreciated.

Then, in September 2006, I flew back to San Francisco, CA. I stayed with a dear friend and was guided to purchase another car. I intuitively heard to look at a specific foreign car dealership. However, to my surprise, I found my Ford minivan in their resale lot. As in the past automobile purchases, the beautiful, well-kept car was on sale and had very low mileage. I definitely have car angels, too.

Then I was guided to move for three months to famous Ashland, Oregon. The angelic journey also took me to Puerto Rico, New Mexico, Florida, and northern and southern California. I seemed to always be sent to great tourist places, such as Santa Fe, Marin County, Palm Springs, and Santa Cruz.

Once I find a place to settle in, I focus on getting to know the area and offering my classes, workshops, and private sessions. I also financially support myself with international telephone sessions. Writing what I have learned and continue to discover is also ongoing and enjoyable.

One way I connect with the communities is to attend the New Thought Churches. I often find people there I can relate to and who are interested in my lectures and other services.

Like many other people I know, my biological family has not chosen the same metaphysical and spiritual path. Of course, I wish they would walk with me. Can you relate?

However, I have let go of my attachment to my relatives understanding or accepting my way of life. I honor all people's paths, and do what feels right to me, no matter what anyone says or does.

I once read a wonderful definition of enlightenment. It is simply to do what you are called to do and allow others to react as they choose. I have the courage, trust, and faith that I will connect with people who will support me on my spiritual path. Wherever I am, I find friends who I can communicate with on this level of consciousness. I call them my "spiritual family."

Each time I move, I have to give away some of the things that I have accumulated, and then creatively pack everything back into my car. I follow my intuition to know what to keep and what to enjoy giving to others. I pray for help to lift the heavy things, and the perfect people shows up.

I must admit that the moving has not always been easy. However, it sure has been a great adventure and spiritual journey. My personality loves to explore new places and meet more like-minded people.

Wherever I go, I think, "I wonder who God wants me to meet and serve and who will serve me." I also constantly listen to my intuition to discover what my next project is and how to proceed with my divine services. I stay tuned to "GOD radio." When people say they don't get that station, I reply, "Yes, you do!"

I live vertically instead of horizontally. For example, when I need a haircut, I ask my angelic guides where to go. I am then guided to the perfect hairdresser. The same process works for everything I need and want. It makes getting settled in a new community much easier.

I imagine that sometime in the future, I will have a home base again. I have no idea where I will settle. However, I do know that I will be wherever it is for my highest good and the good of all. I also know that as I continue to follow my spirit, my intuition, life is an exciting adventure as a loyal angel on call!

As I am preparing this book for the second printing in 2020, I am happy to share that the angles did guide me to a home base. I am very grateful to be living in San Jose, California, in a beautiful, quiet home near my family.

My trust and faith has kept me safe and healthy. I am still helping many people as a psychotherapist, author, psychic, and spiritual teacher. In fact, this book is the textbook for my Spiritual Masters Training. As always, I am happily serving as an *angel on call!*

PART II

One of God's Scribes

8: *Spirituality Versus Religion*

This section is filled with pathways to love and enlightenment. The important insights and transformational exercises have helped me walk in ease and grace, joy and love, trust and faith, and surrender to service. Many of my clients and students have greatly benefited from the wisdom I channeled from the beings of the light. I am grateful for the opportunity to support you in your spiritual journey to enlightenment!

Do you think that spirituality and religion are synonymous? I used to think that they were, but as I learned more, I discovered there are major differences. I realized that you can be spiritual and religious, spiritual and not religious, or religious and not spiritual. That may seem confusing. I will explain.

As I was counseling many clients, I became aware of only two basic emotions, love and fear. The loved-based emotions include compassion, forgiveness, caring, kindness, and unconditional love, which is true love because there are no conditions. Whereas fear-based emotions include control, guilt, anger, abuse, and passive and active aggression.

It is also helpful to understand that we have four basic parts: mental, emotional, physical, and spiritual. Our human personalities are composed of our mental, emotional, and physical parts. They make us unique. Our spiritual part is our higher-self, our all-good, all-knowing, unconditional loving part. It is also known as our God-self. We can connect with our spiritual truths through our intuition.

Therefore, spirituality comes from our spiritual part. When we commit to being honest, kind, caring, loving and accepting of others and ourselves, we are acting from our spiritual part. We have integrity, create win-win solutions, see everyone as equals and deserving of life, liberty, and the pursuit of happiness, and do what we can to make a positive difference.

For example, I know of a policeman who stopped a truck driver for drunken driving. He knew that if he arrested the middle-aged man, he would lose his job and not be able to support his family. Instead, he drove him home and talked to him about his problem. He also counseled his family. I call him a "spiritual cop." He cared enough to help the man rather than punish him.

Spiritual people support everyone having equal rights. They act considerate and responsible. They believe in the power of positive thinking and take responsibility for their lives. Spirituality means living from love rather than fear.

Where does God or a higher power come into all of this? If someone believes in a divine being that looks like a light or person, it will be a loving one that supports, protects, and provides for them. They feel supported to be their unique selves. Spiritual people accept that God is all-loving, and all-powerful, and wants them to be happy, healthy, abundant, and successful. They often speak directly to God, instead of having a person relay God's messages to them. Or, they are spiritual and religious because they have loving spiritual leaders and books that support them living from love and acceptance.

Spiritual people do not have any dogma or rules except spiritual truths. An example is Karma, which is simply the process of cause and effect. We create future karma continually with every thought and action. For example, if you are cruel to other people, you will probably experience people being mean back. Your kindness will be rewarded with a return of kindness.

On the other hand, religion has a dogma and a human being interpreting their God's messages. As we all know, human beings have fears and they can alter the information, consciously or unconsciously. Religious books were translated by man throughout the ages. The information can be loving or fear-based. It is my belief that if it is loving and supportive, then it is spiritual. However, if it is preaching guilt, control, superiority, judgment of others who are different, and believing only their truth is right, it is not spiritual. If it is teaching that you are sinful and here to suffer and struggle, it is not spiritual.

I do not believe that God tries to control us. God honors our free will and wants us to be happy as any healthy parent would. "Joy and laughter are signs of God's presence." I believe that God gave us the proverb, "Do unto others as you want others to do unto you." Honor and accept everyone, and allow them to live their lives as they choose. Spiritual people live and let live. They see everyone as equals and support freedom and liberty for all. They live from love!

9: *Cosmic Partnership*

Have you ever been happy and felt proud for some wonderful thing that happened that you predicted and helped to bring about? Did you ever have anyone dampen your experience by saying, "You didn't do it; God did?"

When that happened to me, I felt terrible. My friends were concerned about their washed-away road. The entrance to their property had to be repaired in order for them to offer winter workshops at their non-profit center. I reassured them that donations would supply the needed funds.

One Sunday morning in October, a contractor that my friends had previously contacted unexpectedly knocked on their door. He explained that he happened to be in the neighborhood and thought he would stop by to give an estimate, and to offer them the option of fixing the road Monday or in a few months.

Miraculously, the much-needed donation appeared that evening. The next day the crew "paved the way" to the center. The crackling sound of my tires rubbing against the gravel was music to my ears. I was especially excited because I had been instrumental in connecting the generous donor with my friends.

A few weeks later, I was telling a male friend of mine, "I'm more powerful than I had realized. I predicted that the road would be repaired with donations in time for the winter months, and it was." My bubble burst when my friend replied, "You didn't do it. God did." However, I recovered as I thought about it and said, "God alone couldn't do it. It took my friends who own the center, me, the donor, and the contractor with his crew to complete the project. We were all important pieces to the puzzle."

It became very clear to me that God needed us as much as we needed God. Working together as a team, we can accomplish many great things on this earth plane. For example, I believe that God wants me to write this so that you can receive the message—the message being how important you are in the design of things. In order for God to serve through me, the Divine Being needs my body to sit in front of the computer, my mind to put this idea into literary form, and my emotions to get excited about doing it. Together, we make a great team.

Where does the issue of humility fit into all of this? I still do feel humble because I know that my creative ideas come ultimately from God.

Ironically, that night I received a phone call from another friend who was reaching out to me for emotional support. As I shared this new concept with her, she also felt relieved. In the past she had been taught that she was nothing and that God was everything. That negative, limited thinking caused her to feel unworthy and unimportant. On the contrary, I believe that we are very worthy and very important. We are the co-creators of our lives. We are truly in partnership with the all-loving, all-knowing Divine energy, in whatever form that takes for you.

So stand tall and proud and take credit for your contributions on this planet. And also know that God is always there to work with you and through you. What a divine experience—A Cosmic Partnership.

10: *Cosmic Mission*

Why are we here? Have we come to play the role of husband, wife, parent, teacher, healer, etc.? Are we here to love, play, and experience life to the fullest? What is our primary mission on this planet?

I have pondered that question many times. I used to believe that I came here to "save the world" from its frightful destruction. With world peace as my vision, I was driven to reach as many people as possible through teaching, counseling, books, tapes, CDs, lectures, workshops, and the media. I was determined to help people love themselves and feel their inner peace—their greatest contribution to world peace.

My logical mind told me that I was succeeding in my life mission. But my low energy and chronic physical pain caused me to have some doubts. I felt miserable! All the stress I put myself through resulted in tight muscles, spinal misalignment, and troubled organs and glands. I suffered with many allergic reactions from foods and toxic environments.

Even though I hated giving up coffee, cheesecake, pizza, and other favorites, deep down I knew it was all perfect. I realized that in order for me to accomplish my primary mission, I had to "clean up my act." My spiritual part reminded me that I chose to walk in the light. During my morning meditations, I surrendered to my service and asked my guides and God, "What would you like me to do today?" The answer was always the same: "Beloved one, be in peace."

Noticing all the pain and misery in the world, I realized that earth is like a remedial class. We all flunked self-love and we came back to get it! And only when we feel that self-love can we experience inner peace.

Now I am clear that my divine purpose for being here is for my soul growth. My cosmic mission is to live on this third-dimensional (fear-based) planet with a fifth-dimensional (love-based) consciousness. My mission is to transcend my will and to allow the all-loving God to work through me.

My mind knew that concept before, but now my soul experiences it. Now I am focusing on the essence of unconditional love and joy and not on the form. My lesson here is to "love myself to peace," to be in that love space no matter what I or others are doing or not doing. It is to transcend what my mind thinks or understands and to remain centered, totally accepting whatever happens as divine.

This is my most difficult challenge. I know that I am succeeding when I maintain a love space or return to it quickly, even after a personal disappointment or upset. I feel so much joy and peace when I overcome my fears and return to my faith.

Since I have totally surrendered to living my life from love and light, I am much happier and healthier. I need much less from the outside world to feel good, and I no longer drive myself to be so goal oriented. I still have the same vision of world peace, and I am still committed to reaching as many people as I can in my lifetime. But now I am coming from love and not fear. Now I am doing it God's way.

The focus of my accomplishments each day is not what I do but how much I feel love, joy, and inner peace. It feels wonderful to be crystal clear about why I am here—about my cosmic mission.

On this earth plane. For example, I believe that God wants me to write this so that you can receive the message—the message being how important you are in the design of things. In order for God to serve through me, the Divine Being needs my body to sit in front of the computer, my mind to put this idea into literary form, and my emotions to get excited about doing it. Together, we make a great team.

Where does the issue of humility fit into all of this? I still do feel humble because I know that my creative ideas come ultimately from God.

Ironically, that night I received a phone call from another friend who was reaching out to me for emotional support. As I shared this new concept with her, she also felt relieved. In the past she had been taught that she was nothing and that God was everything. That negative, limited thinking caused her to feel unworthy and unimportant. On the contrary, I believe that we are very worthy and very important. We are the co-creators of our lives. We are truly in partnership with the all-loving, all-knowing Divine energy, in whatever form that takes for you.

So stand tall and proud and take credit for your contributions on this planet. And also know that God is always there to work with you and through you. What a divine experience—A Cosmic Partnership.

11: *"Intergalactic Peace Corp"*

It was a misty Sunday morning and I had just listened to a tape by a spiritual teacher. The fresh air called out to me, and I left my cabin to bathe in it. Feeling great reverence and spiritually high, I walked the hills in great peace. The stillness inside of me matched the quiet all around me.

Exhilarated, I returned home and, as if in a trance, proceeded to sit in front of the computer. The view of the mountains through the window was awe inspiring. My fingers started moving on the keyboard as quickly as they could. Less than an hour later, I read what had transpired. I was surprised how deeply touched I felt by the truth, the beauty, and the depth of the words. I knew it was going to be one of my articles. In fact, it is my favorite!

Do you ever feel as though your drum beats to a different tune than the people around you? Have you possibly had the painful thought that you do not belong here, and that you want to go home? Are you sometimes plagued by a nagging thought that you are here for a purpose, but you do not know what it is?

If you answered "yes" to any of the above questions, you may be a member of the "Intergalactic Peace Corp." If that idea surprises you, then congratulate yourself for being successful in deluding yourself about your truth, because that was the first part of your mission.

If you are continuing to read this, you are probably one of the courageous volunteers who came to serve at this time. The main reason you had enlisted as part of the intergalactic team on this earth mission was because of your great love for this planet. Besides having the sincere desire, you felt confident that your much needed skills and abilities were an important part of the Divine Plan.

You realized that in the process of giving, you would be receiving by escalating your own soul evolvement. Your commitment to reincarnate also offered you an opportunity to clear some negative karma that you had accumulated during your previous lifetimes on earth.

You felt honored when God asked you to join this momentous mission. With a sense of adventure, great joy, and excitement, you said, "Yes!" and you proudly took your spiritual vows.

Then you decided who your parents would be based on your karma with them and their ability to help you learn your chosen lessons. When you were conceived by your mother, the veils came tumbling down and you forgot who you were. This was necessary so that you could be a part of the human race, in a sense infiltrate it, and make changes from within.

You might have had second thoughts when you started feeling the pain of the fear-based illusions embedded in this third dimension. Coming from the fifth dimension or higher, where there is only love and light, you forgot how difficult this planet could be. Being very sensitive, you probably heard or sensed negative thoughts from your parents and others and felt the negative energy transferred from your mother to you through the umbilical cord as you floated in the womb.

Losing touch with the fact that you were supported by many other spiritual beings from the light, including God, you fell into the illusion of darkness, of separation. It was frightening to think that you were all alone and possibly not even wanted by your parents, or deserving of being born. But you courageously persisted and survived the birth trauma. When you were greeted by blinding bright lights and a painful smack on your buttocks, you may have been convinced that it was not safe here on earth.

If your parents were unable to express their love, your drama intensified. As you were growing up, if they were critical, or too busy to tend to you, you probably decided that you were not good enough, important, lovable, worthy, or intelligent. If they shouted or spanked you, you were convinced that you must be bad. If they were in pain, you most likely blamed yourself, felt guilty, and absorbed their negative energy. When they demanded that you be a certain way, you locked up the real you and pretended to be someone else. These survival tactics worked, but you were miserable inside.

Your soap opera probably began early in life, and you can pride yourself on the roles you played. You did such a good job that you could be a candidate for an Academy Award. The only trouble is, you forgot it was all an act. You forgot who the real you is.

Now is the time to wake up. Now is the time to move on to the second phase of the mission. Let go of all your fear-based illusions. Let the decorative stage curtain fall to indicate the end of the human drama phase of your mission. Applaud yourself for a job well done.

Reverse the process, and now forget the false limitations you learned on this planet and recall the true, unlimited reality. Let the veils lift so that you can remember who you are and why you came here. Turn inward, heal the inner child, and realize that you are lovable, worthy, important, good enough, intelligent, and a good person. In fact, you are a beautiful child of God. Accept your oneness with all and experience your spark of light. Ignite your spiritual flames and let them fill you with love and light.

Reconnect with your unlimited spirit (that is who you really are), put yourself in the driver's seat, and tell your mind, body, and emotions that you love them and need them all to function on this planet, but that you are now in control. Courageously explore and express your unique skills and gifts. When your life flows, and you love what you are doing, you will know that you are impeccably in tune with your divine service. Let your light shine and your Intergalactic Peace Corp teammates will find you and support you. Ask for all that you need and be open to receiving it.

Understand that the people who you feel have hurt you have done their job well by helping you to experience the pain of humanity. Forgive them, and forgive yourself for buying into the limitations and feeling like a victim. Accept them where they are, honor their free will, and avoid trying to change them or demanding that they go with you. Realize that they always did the best they could with the information they had—they were controlled by their distorted perceptions of themselves and others.

Acknowledge that their spirit also knows the Divine Plan, and that they have gone as far as they can. Imagine that they are passing you the baton, and now it is your turn to make the final stretch to the finish line. They are counting on you to take them back to the light. Since we are all connected, all divine spirits, as you free yourself of the fear based-illusions, you are helping to liberate others.

As you succeed in your personal transformation from darkness into light, from fear into love, you can truly be one of the glorious midwives of this beautiful planet. Earth, a divine living organism, is also now being transformed, liberated, and freed from fear-based illusions. You incarnated during these exciting times in order to assist in this incredible shift, this planetary rebirth into the light. This is the mission that you exuberantly opted to serve in. With grace and humility, walk forward into the known— your spirit knows exactly what is happening, what you will be doing, where you are going, and how you will get there. Surrender to faith and listen inside for your guidance.

It is safe to come out now and be all that you are. Now is the time to acknowledge your magnificence, your peaceful power, your God-self. With joy, love, and light, follow your unique path without hesitation, and make your peaceful contribution as part of the honored "Intergalactic Peace Corp."

Can you relate to this? I certainly did. It was definitely clear to me that I had joined this divine peace corp. I felt honored and privileged, and ready to embark on my chosen service.

12: *A Classical Walk-in*

"Put your seat belt on," Cindy heard intuitively. Fortunately for her, she paid attention to her inner wisdom. Soon after the fifty-five-year-old petite woman buckled her belt, the truck in front of her stopped without warning. She quickly glanced into the rear view mirrors and saw oncoming cars in each lane. The accident seemed to be unavoidable. There was no way out, so Cindy braced herself for the crash.

The next thing she knew, a policeman was approaching her car with a crowbar. Cindy realized that she must have been unconscious. By some miracle, she felt sore but calm. Her thoughts were, "Something is different, very different. What has happened to me?" Cindy's little car was totaled and people at the scene wondered how she could have walked out alive. After answering many questions, the bruised and shaken woman told the policeman she was okay and just wanted to go home.

The next day, Cindy was aware of feeling very different, like a butterfly coming out of a cocoon. It was a mystery—her personality felt changed. She was used to meditating with the angels, so she asked, "What is happening to me?" The angels responded, "Cindy went home. Another being named Mary now resides in your body. As incredible as it may sound, this is Spirit's way of transforming a soul to its highest honor. Welcome to Earth, Mary."

Cindy thought that she must be making this all up. But over the next few days everything began changing; all her ideas, thoughts, and habits. Her whole outlook on life changed. She felt as though she had been through a whirlwind.

That is an accurate description of what Cindy had experienced. Unconsciously she had made an agreement with a higher spirit to come in and utilize her body for a vehicle on Planet Earth. Cindy had wanted to leave, and this was an excellent way to continue to serve even after her spirit left her body.

A walk-in is an efficient way God created to help higher beings come in quickly instead of going through the natural birth process and many years of growth and training. In this way, almost immediately they can begin to do their light work. Especially now, during the Age of Aquarius, many are needed to assist the masses to expand their consciousness—to live more in their hearts and create peace on earth. Many people on earth have had, and continue to have, this divine experience.

Like buying a used car, a walk-in takes the body as it is. It takes a while for the new spirit to heal the body. In Cindy's case, the healing was taking place very quickly. Since I had previously assisted her with other problems as a counselor, psychic, and spiritual healer, she trusted me to help her understand, accept, and integrate the new energies. Within a few days, her chronic maladies were dissipating. She was already decreasing her medication for high blood pressure and allergies.

It was understandable that Cindy was confused because she was aware of some of her old thoughts and behaviors and yet she felt like a brand new person. She began to accept that her old self was no longer present. Mary had taken residence within her being and she felt more comfortable with her new self every day. This new presence was obviously stronger, braver, happier, and more grounded.

For example, when she entered a cleaning store, two large German Shepherds started barking. Her old personality would have panicked, because she had previously been bitten by such a dog. However, she remained calm, gently raised her hand, and smiled as she said in a loving voice, "It's okay." To her surprise, and that of the owner, the dogs quieted down.

Cindy was brought up by very loving but overprotective parents. Her mother's fears and worries had rubbed off on her in many ways. Cindy was afraid to drive very far from home, but Mary drove much farther and even in the pouring rain. She also found herself speaking up to people, something she never did before. Being assertive was definitely not one of her previous traits.

63

Mary continued to have many new experiences that were very much out of her old character. Cindy's introverted personality was no more. A strong, active extrovert was quickly evolving. Mary's vision of her service was expanding to being a healer. In a meditation, the angels showed her flashes of her new role.

The neighbors and friends who dropped in to check on her all said that she looked very different and even better than before the accident. When Mary looked into the mirror, she also saw an unfamiliar face. This part of the change was a little scary and eerie. Fortunately, the angels kept whispering into her ears comforting and reassuring words.

Mary recalled Cindy telling her friends before the accident that she felt she would be going Home after she completed her twelfth and final tape of a series. Now she realized that Cindy was totally fulfilled when she "died" and Mary walked-in.

Looking back, Mary realized that Cindy's personality was like that of a loving mouse. But Mary was flying high on the back of an eagle. Her expansive feelings were exhilarating and exciting. Mary felt courageous and ready to fulfill her new mission. Cindy had gone as far as she could. She graciously passed the baton on to Mary who was ready to move full speed ahead. She smiled and thought, "God works in mysterious but wondrous ways!"

13: *Warrior Versus Spiritual Warrior*

One Saturday night, my friends and I were invited to watch a wonderful slide show about sacred places. It was presented by a young man who sincerely wanted to make a difference. I appreciated his cause and efforts. However, I left feeling mostly his anger and judgments of others. I had compassion for his pain, and realized that many others, including me, have sabotaged our good intentions in this negative way. The experience inspired me to write the article about the difference between a warrior and a spiritual warrior, and about serving as a loving, all-powerful, spiritual warrior.

It feels like a dilemma! Many of us see so much that angers and frighten us, and we know that it is not right to abuse anybody or anything. We feel our hearts crying, "It's supposed to be different!" Deep inside we know how to honor our beautiful Mother Earth, brothers and sisters, and ourselves. We know the universal values of honoring and respecting all. We want so much to make it all better. We want to make a difference, but the question is, "How"?

Naturally, we are tempted to pick up our swords. We have had many lifetimes as a warrior. We know how to use our might. We see and hear so much violence in the media, on our streets, and possible even in our homes. Isn't that the way? It is familiar.

With our angry "sword" in hand we attack others, verbally and possibly even physically. We'll beat them into submission. We'll knock some sense into them. We'll tell them off. After all, we know the truth. They are wrong, so wrong! They are destroying the world. Because of them we have no peace. We think that we are on the good side, and they represent evil.

Down deep we are terrified. We know that if the world is not saved, we will also die with the masses. With personal survival at stake, we clench our teeth, tighten our muscles, and set on our path to teach "the way."

With so much fear and anger we drive ourselves -- often pushing our bodies beyond their human limitations. We tell ourselves we are struggling for a good cause. After all, we are running out of time. The world must wake up now or perish!

To our dismay, many of our efforts do not appear to be making a difference. We have done so much, and yet we still feel so empty and powerless inside. Nothing truly seems to satisfy us -- at least for more than a day or two. Nothing seems to meet our expectations. What's wrong? We study so much. We do so much and try so hard. Why aren't we feeling fulfilled? What needs to change?

One day we have an awakening. Maybe it was ignited by a dream, an insight, or a word we heard or read. Maybe we had to get seriously sick or hurt to be knocked down off our high horse, get quiet and listen inside. Maybe the key, the answer, has been inside all the time. We know the TRUTH.

We hear the awesome whisper inside telling us, "It's time to trade in your warrior sword for your powerful 'weapon' of love and light. Change comes from example, from your 'beingness' more than from your 'doingness.' Be the person you wish others to be. Be loving and accepting of all. Have compassion for people's pain, and judge them not or you shall be judged. Heal thyself and you shall make a powerful contribution to the world. Have the courage to face yourself, to explore your own personal pain."

Did you feel loved and accepted by your parents? Do you feel good enough, worthy, and important? Can you look in the mirror and say from your heart, "I love you?" Are you in peace with your parents, siblings, and other significant people in your life, past and present? If not, are you possibly projecting your pain with them onto others?

Can you do nothing and feel peacefully powerful? Do you have faith that a higher source is there to guide, support, and protect you and others? Are you aware that love and light are your power and protection? Are you willing to meet negativity with love and compassion? Can you walk your talk?"

These are the issues I also had to consider. My angelic guides have helped me transform from a warrior to a spiritual warrior. They taught me that my most powerful "weapon" is to imagine God's unlimited pink light of love flowing down into the top of my head and into the center of my chest (heart Chakra). This divine action heals my heart and helps me be in my love space. Then I beam the pink light unconditionally to the heart center of anyone I feel is in anger, fear or pain, or hurtful to others or themselves. They told me that my power ends there, because people have free will to take it in or not. However, what they choose to do does not concern me, because there is a law of the Universe that what you put out comes back.

I have used this spiritual process many times with great success. I no longer try to convince people of anything. I merely share my truth unconditionally in a loving way. My students and clients have also expressed the many positive results they have experienced when they dealt with people as a spiritual warrior. When we open ourselves up to the peaceful power of living in love and sending love and light, we serve the world as a spiritual master, and we make a major difference.

14: *Twelve Steps to Enlightenment*

How exciting it is to live in the light, in love and joy. How wonderful it is to be enlightened and to be free of ignorance, prejudice, and fear. This is our reason for being here on Planet Earth. This is our divine purpose.

To live in ease and grace on this beautiful Mother Earth can be a challenge, because earth is on the third dimension. That means that it is a planet of polarities—dark and light, fear and love.

How courageous we are to reincarnate, to live out our human dramas, and to rise above them. Once we transcend our issues, we can live on this third dimension with a fifth-dimension consciousness. (The fourth dimension is the astral plane.) Living from this higher consciousness, in love and light, is what is truly meant by "heaven on earth."

Everyone can achieve a level of enlightenment. When you accelerate to that level, you know that you are *on* the Planet Earth but not *from* the planet. You realize that your very essence is love and light. As one of my bumper stickers says, we are "Just visiting this planet."

We all have a spirit called our higher self, which is located above our heads. Since we are love and light, our spirits are from the fifth dimension or higher. That is why we can say that we are all one. We are all love and light.

Everyone also has a soul, which sits, in the center of our chests near our hearts. It represents our unique personalities because it has cell memories of all our experiences and the decisions we made from them. The goal is to clear away and overcome all of our negative decisions so that we can open our hearts, feel love, and be one with ourselves—our higher selves. Only then can we live in peace and joy, and that is our greatest contribution to world peace.

Since we are all one, when we overcome our fears and live from love and acceptance (unconditional love), we affect many others. It works as a ripple effect, just as one stone thrown in the lake causes movement for quite a distance.

This is in line with the Hundredth Monkey concept. Scientists observed monkeys on an island off Japan adopting a new behavior—washing the potatoes that were their staple food. They noticed that when a large percentage of the monkeys made the change in behavior, monkeys on several other islands automatically made the same change—even though they did not have any direct contact with the other monkeys.

As you can see, it is wonderful and powerful for us and others to become enlightened. What we think, feel, do, and say does make a difference.

This chapter is a guideline. It offers twelve steps to assist you in your transformation into the light. I recommend that you read all of it through and then let your higher self or intuition guide you to focus on the exercise(s) that will serve you at this time.

I offer a few words of support. Be compassionate and patient with yourself. Live one day at a time. Focus on your accomplishments and the present moment instead of the future. When you live in the now, you are constantly shaping your future. Because you have free will, you can change the course of your life at any time. See the humor in situations, and enjoy the journey called life!

STEP ONE: INTENT

The first of the twelve steps is to declare your intent. Since your thoughts and words are magnetic, you will draw to you whatever you think and say. Therefore, if your intent is to be enlightened, the process will automatically begin.

To declare your heart's desire, it is helpful to lie down on your back, breathe deeply, and relax with your palms up and legs apart. This open position helps you surrender to your divine power. Then your goal can be stated as follows, or with a similar declaration: "My intent is to live my life from my spirit, from love and joy."

Then you can say some affirmations (positive statements) to support your intent. For example: "I surrender to my higher self. I accept all positive support from this planet and above to help me become enlightened."

It is also a good idea to write your intent on a piece of paper with colorful magic markers and place it somewhere where you will often see it. Some examples are: in your wallet, on your bathroom mirror, desk, dresser, refrigerator, or door.

Feel free to change the words to suit your desires. Speak your intent from your heart and be prepared for miracles to occur. Be aware of omens or signs. For example, if a book falls off a library or bookstore shelf, examine it closely. It may be your higher self guiding you to the perfect book for you at the time.

Remember that there are no coincidences, and everything that happens has a purpose. Look for messages and you will find them. Now you can move on to step two so that you can learn ways to clearly communicate with your higher self.

STEP TWO: INTUITION

Everyone is intuitive. We all receive valid information from our higher selves in one or more of the following ways:

1. Clairsentience - feelings in the gut

2. Clairaudience - inner words that we hear

3. Clairvoyance - images seen through the third eye in the center of the forehead

4. Telepathy - a deep knowing

Some other ways we can communicate with spirit are:

1. Say a "yes" statement and then a "no" statement, and each time focus inside and be aware of your body's reaction. You will instantly know your truth. It is like trying on a dress or suit.

You do not know if it fits until you try it on. Say the following two statements, and pay attention to how your body feels to discover your truth.

"My name is _____." (Example: My name is Helene.)

"My name is _____." (Example: My name is Mary.)

2. Have your left pinky and thumb touching. Put your right thumb and second finger between your left pinky and thumb. Say, "My name is (your name)," and try to push the left fingers apart with the right ones. Since that is a true statement, your left pinky and thumb will remain strong and continue to touch each other. Then say, "My name is (a different name)," and your fingers will be weak and separate because that is not a true statement. Your body knows the truth. If your muscles are strong, that always indicate a positive response (yes), and if they are weak, the answer is negative one (no). If it does not seem to work for you, try switching hands.

3. Stretch your arm out straight to the side (shoulder height). Ask someone to press your arm down as you ask the same two questions about your name from exercise number two. Try to resist their downward pressure. The strongest person in the world cannot keep their arm straight out if the answer to their question is "no."

We are constantly receiving messages from our higher self. All we need to do is to be quiet and tune in to this valuable information. It is like turning the dial on the radio to the "I" station, your intuition, your true self. This is probably the most important information you will ever receive, and it is free and always available. Your intuition can save your life, help you find that perfect job, house, or parking space.

Intelligence is your ability to learn with your mind left brain), but intuition (right brain) is wisdom. I have counseled many clients who were very bright. Their minds were extremely active and filled with information. However, since they were blocking their intuition, they lacked wisdom to live in love and joy. Their hard work never seemed to make them feel fulfilled.

What does make us happy? *I define true success as an internal feeling of fulfillment, peace, and power, which comes from being who you are and doing what you want to do.* Notice that it is not found by focusing out there in the third dimensional world. Success is not felt when you are motivated to do things because you feel a need to prove something to yourself or others, or to please your parents, etc.

The pathway to happiness is to follow your intuition. Fulfillment is only felt when you put your higher self in the driver's seat and your mind, body, and emotions carry out your unique spiritual desires.

For example, one morning during my meditation, my higher self sent me an unexpected message in a flash. Suddenly I had a vision of a chapter entitled, "Twelve Steps to Enlightenment." I heard the words, "Begin to write the much needed information today."

I felt very excited about this new adventure. My body took me to the computer and my mind operated my sophisticated machine. Since I only had a title, I typed that on the screen first. Then I quieted my mind and allowed my intuition to take over. I trusted that my spirit would write the divine information through me. So far you have read what had effortlessly flowed through me in just a few hours. What fun!

In summary, explore ways that you can heighten your intuition, your communication with your higher self. Your mind does not have to figure it all out, or even know what will be happening. If you stay tuned in, your spirit will offer you all the information and guidance you need. Your spirit will help you fulfill your heart's desires, which will be for the good of all. Then you can enjoy your life, feel great satisfaction, and experience true success.

STEP THREE: MEDITATION

Meditation is one way to experience inner peace, because you shift into an altered state of consciousness, which is beyond the mind. This helps you feel rested, and it calms the mind so that you can hear messages from your higher self.

You can begin this process by again stating your INTENT. In this case, it is to choose to meditate. Then decide on a time and place where you can be quiet and turn inward. Most meditations are done with your eyes closed and sitting in a comfortable place. It is helpful to meditate at least twenty minutes, twice a day. However, do your best to schedule the time to have silent moments for as long as you desire. It is often recommended to meditate in the morning when you arise and again in the late afternoon. You will probably find it a wonderful way to unwind from the day after work and feel refreshed so that you can enjoy the evening.

There are many ways to meditate. Some people learn a mantra, a sound that helps them shift into other dimensions. Others keep repeating a word like love or peace. Another method is to be the observer of your thoughts, let them pass through your mind and focus on your breathing. You can also visualize images that help you feel peaceful, such as the beach, mountain top, forest, or meadow.

Another way to meditate is to listen to music that helps you shift into the higher dimensions. You can choose to be guided by a tape or person through a peaceful visualization journey. Still another suggestion is to quietly walk in nature and observe the scenery. Explore the perfect way(s) to meditate that help(s) you calm your mind and feel a deep level of inner peace.

STEP FOUR: MIND

Our basic essence is our spirit, and when we decide to experience life on Planet Earth we take on human parts known as bodies, minds, and emotions. When we are born, our spirit is still in control and we only know how to be in the moment. Notice how beautiful, real, spontaneous, and flowing babies are. Since they are still in an innocent, pure state of being, they are not thinking or planning what they will do next week or even tomorrow. Babies live totally in the now and can spend hours being fascinated by their toes.

When they are born, some of the veils have come down so that they can be on this earth plane. However, their spirit, their pure self, is being expressed through their body, mind, and emotions. When babies are scared or hurt, they cry. They do not have the ability yet to block their true feelings, to pretend that everything is fine. At that age there is no agenda to impress anyone or convince others that they are okay.

However, children believe that they are the center of the universe and that they are responsible for everything that happens. Their young minds are capable of making decisions based on their experiences, and a feeling follows the belief. Therefore, fears are a result of negative decisions.

For example, when I guided many clients back to their childhood, I discovered that when young children experience their parents' fighting, they think that they are responsible, and decide that they must be bad. This negative decision becomes part of their programming, or life script. This limiting thought sets them up for a lot of pain and disappointment in their lives. Since they think and feel that they are bad, they will punish themselves by not allowing themselves to be healthy, happy, or successful. They believe that they deserve to suffer and unconsciously sabotage all their efforts to reach their desired goals.

As I counseled hundreds of clients, I discovered that no matter what drama was going on in the clients' lives, the cause of the problem was always the negative decisions that they had made from their experiences early in life. For example, "I am not okay, worthy, important, good enough, or lovable. I am a bad person." All of these negative thoughts caused an emotional response we call FEAR (False Evidence Appearing Real).

The process I developed called HART: Holistic and Rapid Transformation (previously known as Creative Therapy), helps many people heal themselves of these self-defeating thoughts. I ask them to close their eyes and then guide them back to the time they made the negative decisions that were running their lives. I encourage them to express the painful feelings that were associated with the negative thought (fear, anger, guilt, etc.). Once they feel better, I suggest that they burn away the scene with a laser beam, and then create (visualize or sense) a positive experience so that they can make a positive decision, which will help them feel good about themselves, and allow themselves to be happy, healthy, and successful.

74

When the client is able to accept the truth that, "You are only responsible for what you say or do," and that, "What people say or do is a reflection of them and not of you," they feel separate from and not responsible for the other people's thoughts, feelings, or actions. When they realize that they are okay, worthy, important, good enough, lovable, and a good person, they are "free to fly."

One powerful technique that I share with clients to help them shift their negative thoughts to positive ones I call the S.O.S. process. It is based on my discovery that most of our emotional pain results from our mistaken belief that what happens or does not happen is a statement or reflection of us. This process helps us to separate ourselves from the event and to understand that what happens is merely something to observe.

Whenever you want to call for help because you feel angry, scared, hurt, etc., try the following S.O.S. exercise.

Ask yourself: What am I telling myself? Then use the three steps below to help you uncover the negative thought or cause of your pain.

1. The event = I am not okay.
2. The event = the event.
3. I am okay.

Examples:

1. My boss yelled at me = I am not okay (good enough, etc.).
2. My boss yelled at me = my boss yelled at me.
3. I am okay (good enough, etc.).

As you can see, the above process helps you realize the truth that the event is simply the event, and you are okay no matter what anyone says or does. More information is available in my book, *All You Need Is HART! Create Love, Joy and Abundance ~ NOW!*

STEP FIVE: EMOTIONS

There are two basic emotions, love and fear. Every other emotion is an expression of these two. I have learned that fear is the cause of all our problems, and love is always the solution.

For example, if I feel guilty because I do not call my mother as I think should, I feel scared that I am not okay. "Should" means that you are not okay unless you do what you think you *should* do. Since YOU ARE OKAY no matter what you say or do, I suggest that you avoid "shoulding" yourself. If you are "shoulding" yourself, you are probably doing the same thing to others.

Once you realize that you are okay, and you can use the S.O.S. process to release the negative belief and fear, you can choose to call your mother or not and still feel love for yourself.

It is extremely important to deal with your emotions constructively. If you are angry, you can go into your bedroom, hit a soft pillow, and verbally express your deep frustrations. Then get in touch with the underlying feeling of fear, hurt, or powerlessness (you can use the S.O.S. process) and heal yourself.

I believe that there would be world peace if everyone dealt with their anger in this positive way. I believe that wars and all other abuse are caused by a projection of our anger onto others, with the insidious fears of not being okay hiding deep in our unconscious. When our love is running us, and not our fears, we will experience great joy and peace in ourselves and in the world.

We can only be congruently loving (that is feel, speak and act in a loving way) after we constructively release our negative emotions. We are responsible for all of our feelings. Recall from the last chapter that OUR feelings arise from OUR thoughts. No one can make us feel anything.

We will take the same example of the event being your boss yelling at you. If you already think and feel you are bad, unintelligent, not okay, or good enough, you are likely to feel angry, scared, powerless, or frustrated. However, if you think and feel you are a good person, okay, intelligent, and good enough, you are likely to feel compassion for the pain he is experiencing (especially if you realize that anger is a cover-up for fear).

The truth is that your boss is reacting from his negative thoughts and feelings. If he had positive thoughts and feelings about himself, he would act in a positive way. Your boss could then tell you calmly what the problem is and work with you on a win-win solution.

We are okay, but our negative beliefs are often not. If we are scared that we are not okay, then we often behave in negative ways. If anyone hurts themselves or others, it is because they are scared that they are not okay. We are not sick; we are stuck with negative thoughts and feelings about ourselves, others, and the world.

I think that earth is a remedial class, and we all flunked self-love and came back to "get it"! It is time to graduate. It is time to lift the veil, release the illusion that you are not okay, identify with your divine higher self, and acknowledge your pure love and light.

I am totally convinced that we are loving spirits because I never had to teach a client how to love. Once an individual overcame their fear, hurt, anger, etc., the love was underneath, patiently waiting to be expressed.We all know how to love because that is our true essence.

STEP SIX: PHYSICAL BODY

The body is the vehicle for our mind and emotions. It also expresses our thoughts and feelings. The mind makes a decision based on an experience, and that thought triggers an emotional response, which is felt in the body.

For example, if you feel angry when your boss is yelling at you, and you do not express those feelings, then you are likely to go home with a headache. The energy of the anger is blocked in your forehead. If your response to his behavior is fear, you are likely to feel tension in your abdomen and you may have indigestion or a stomach ache.

Counseling people with many different physical complaints taught me that our bodies are literal. If someone does not want to see something, they feel tension in their eyes. Once they express what they are afraid of seeing and resolve the issue, their eyes feel fine.

Simply assisting people to get in touch with what their bodies are trying to tell them by way of an illness or accident helps them heal themselves. The results are exciting.

I highly recommend that when you have any physical complaint, you first uncover what message there is for you before you do the necessary things to heal the physical body. If you just heal the symptom, the physical pain or discomfort, your body may need to create a more serious ailment for you to pay attention to the cause, which is a negative belief of some kind.

It is advisable to also seek holistic doctors or healers. They will see you as a whole person and understand and consider the interdependency of the mind, body, and emotions. Therefore, they will treat what is often the cause (a negative thought and unexpressed emotion), as well as the symptom (the body discomfort).

It is important to take care of your physical body and honor it as the temple of your soul. If you surrender to your spirit, it will guide you to the perfect food, exercises, colors, and fabrics to wear, etc. Listen to your intuition and you will know. You may want to use the techniques listed in Step One (intuition) to receive clear information.

I do not believe that there is any right or wrong diet. You may need different foods at different times based on your health, body type, and activities. However, there are some basic guidelines that are highly recommended for everyone. They include: preparing and eating your food in a loving state (the positive energy will flow into the food), chewing well, eating in moderation, and avoiding sugar as well as chemical preservatives. Drink lots of purified water and avoid foods that upset your digestive system. Take a moment to place your hands over your food to connect your energy to it, and state gratitude and a blessing aloud or silently. I suggest that you make dining a positive and spiritual experience along with everything else in your life.

STEP SEVEN: BALANCE

Balancing our life is necessary to experience health, harmony, and joy. To begin with, we need to balance our four parts: physical, mental, emotional, and spiritual. All of our parts are important and valuable. They all need acceptance, appreciation, and time to be expressed.

You may want to make a schedule for your week. Then ask yourself, "When and how am I expressing my spirit, mind, body, and emotions?"Write down the days and times that each part is active.

For example, to feed your spirit, you may want to meditate daily from 6 to 6:20 a.m. and 5 to 5:20 p.m. Then you can read an enlightening book or listen to a spiritual CD before bedtime.

The mind may have its time to be expressed at your job. Your emotions can safely come out with your friends or intimate partners at lunchtime or in the evenings. Walking quickly or doing yoga and non-impact aerobics in the mornings, lunch time, or before dinner can satisfy your body.

Especially during these intense times, it is vital to our health and well-being to live in balance. Set aside time to play, to re-energize yourself. See the humor in things and laugh often. Give to others and allow yourself to receive.

Try this exercise. Close your eyes and take a few deep breaths. Now visualize a highway in front of you and notice how many lanes are coming towards you and how many are going away from you.

The number of lanes coming toward you is symbolic of how much you are allowing yourself to receive. The lanes gong away from you indicates how much you are giving to others. Ideally, both sides of the highway are even. That means you are giving and receiving equally. If not, do what you can to balance your energy.

For example, if you need to receive more, ask a friend or loved one to do something for you. If you need to give more, do something nice for someone you care about, or even a stranger.

Another aspect of our lives we need to balance is our time alone and our time with others. We are basically social beings and it serves us to be with other supportive people. However, we also need time alone so that we can be quiet, listen to our inner voice, and rejuvenate ourselves.

STEP EIGHT: ENERGY

Everything is energy. Energy and matter are the same. Even traditional science is beginning to acknowledge this idea. A tree, a rock, a table, an automobile, a person, etc., are all different forms, or densities, of energy that vibrate at different frequencies. Love energy is lighter than fear energy because it vibrates faster, at a higher level. Therefore, as you release your fear-based decisions and experience more love in your life, you actually become energetically lighter. In fact, people will intuitively notice your shift because they will sense your love and light.

Another way to increase your flow of high-frequency light energy is through deep breathing. You may want to try the following exercise: Lie down, relax, and close your eyes. Slowly breathe through your nose, and push your abdomen out so that it can be filled with oxygen. Then exhale slowly through your nose or mouth as you pull in your abdomen to force out all the air. As you inhale, visualize or sense white light coming into your body. Then imagine that you are exhaling another color that represents your fears or concerns. Continue this process for as long as it feels comfortable. You are likely to feel lighter, more relaxed, and more peaceful.

This healthy, rejuvenating way of breathing will help you lighten up your body, mind, and emotions. Practice it regularly and it will become a healthy habit that will help you feel calm, heal yourself, and re-energize. Breathe slowly and deeply as much as you can and especially when you are driving, unwinding from a busy day, upset, or stressed. Allow the abundant, peaceful high-frequency energy from the universe to flow through you, to remind you that you are the light.

STEP NINE: SPIRITUAL RELATIONSHIPS

The spiritual purpose of relationships is to help one another on the journey to enlightenment—to overcome our fears and doubts and live in love and joy. In a spiritual relationship, you love your partner unconditionally and want them to be happy and all that they can be. You do not feel responsible for their problems or accomplishments because you realize that you are only responsible for your thoughts, feelings, and actions.

In the ultimate spiritual relationship, you accept that you share your lives for as long as you are supposed to be together. You know that it is perfect whether you are with a person for a few moments or fifty-plus years. Because you remember that your main purpose for being here on Planet Earth is to become enlightened and follow your spirit with no hesitation, you can be free to flow with whatever happens.

Some relationships need to change form at some point (from intimate lovers to friends) because each partner has received what they needed from the other, or they have completed a project that they were both destined to fulfill. Other relationships end because one person has grown to a higher level of self-esteem and the other is choosing to remain in old patterns.

I notice that in my life, and that of my friends and clients, the pain becomes intense when we do not listen to our spirit when it says, "You need to let them go and move on." How more loving and kind it would be for everyone if we could just accept that reality and shift our relationship into a different form.

I recall being very impressed by Don, who loved his wife, Susan, enough to let her go to be with another man because she desired to do so. Don accepted that he was okay and that Susan's next step was to be with and serve with Bill. Don and Susan divorced and transformed their relationship into a wonderful, loving friendship that included her new partner, Bill. Don was very happy for his ex-wife because she was happy and following her spirit.

To create your spiritual relationship, you need to overcome your fears and your third-dimensional thinking, and be committed to loving all of yourself (mind, body, and emotions) unconditionally. Only then can you love another in the same spiritual way.

To connect with your perfect mate, be the person you want your loving partner to be. If you feel in your heart that you are lovable and you act that way, you will attract someone in your life that is also living in that state of consciousness.

In a spiritual relationship, you are both committed to dealing with your issues so that you can realize the truth, which is that you are wonderful, loving, and unlimited beings. You are both willing to continue to raise your self-esteem, communicate constructively, and create win-win solutions. Problems or disharmony are recognized as opportunities for growth—to heal yourselves by developing a deeper level of understanding and love for yourself and your partner.

This basic formula and guidance for spiritual connections applies to all relationships—those with your children, family, friends, co-workers, etc. It is the key to happy and healthy relationships with everyone in your life and can result in great joy, peace, and fulfillment.

STEP TEN: SERVICE

On the pathway to enlightenment, you transform the third-dimensional idea of work to a fifth-dimensional concept called service. Since your goal is to live in a state of higher consciousness, then everything you do for yourself and others is viewed as a service of love.

You may be surprised that service includes things that you do for yourself. The truth is that being self-caring is being selfless and not selfish. Taking care of yourself is a wonderful gift to others and the world. Only when you first take the time to fill your basket can you have something to offer others—things, time, energy, wisdom, and love. We all do everyone a favor by making ourselves number one.

For example, if I take the time to serve myself by resting, meditating, eating properly, exercising, and playing, I have enough energy for my loved ones, clients, and audiences. Once you take care of your own needs and feel good, you can be a patient and loving friend, spouse, sibling, parent, employee, or boss. Not only are you supporting others, but you are also a natural healer. In my opinion, a healer is anyone who helps you feel better about yourself. Since love is the healing power, any time someone you are with is in that high state of consciousness, you automatically receive a healing.

For instance, when I am eating in a restaurant where the chef and server are in a state of love, I experience a healing. I leave the restaurant feeling physically and emotionally fulfilled. I feel a deeper level of self-love and acceptance because they have fed me with love.

You make a difference on the planet, not necessarily by what you are doing, but by the state of consciousness you are in when you offer your services. I recall feeling wonderful every time I opened my mailbox. I doubt that the mailman was consciously aware that he was a healer in his humble service. I am convinced that he loved delivering mail to the people on his route because I felt it.

In summary, take care of yourself first and give to others and yourself from your heart. Express your gratitude, and view everything you do as an honor, as an opportunity to serve, and to spread love and light.

STEP ELEVEN: ABUNDANCE

The concept of abundance, of having more than enough, is a spiritual one because it comes from an unlimited belief. As we rise above our third- dimensional, limited thinking and live from fifth-dimensional unlimited beliefs, we can create all that we need easily and effortlessly.

For example, I wanted to install another telephone in my office. However, when I called the telephone company in Sedona, Arizona, they informed me that there would be no lines available in my area for about eight months and placed me on the waiting list.

Learning to live in faith, I let go and trusted that all was in divine order—that when I truly needed the extra line, it would appear. Three months later, my intuition told me to call the telephone company and check in on the status of my order. When I connected with the person who had my papers on her desk she reiterated that there would be no lines for another five months. I said, "I was told that before, but I thought that maybe we could create a miracle."

After some moments of silence, the representative said in a perplexed voice, "It looks as though you are scheduled to receive another phone line in three weeks." I laughed and replied, "I knew that we could create a miracle!" Of course, the second phone line was installed just when I needed it.

Another example is when I had huge expenses that resulted in a shortage of cash flow, and I did not know how I was going to pay my next month's rent. I said, "Okay Spirit, you will have to create a miracle here." Then, with ease and grace, I went about my normal day's activities. The phone started ringing and numerous clients called from all over the country. Three people from Phoenix, Arizona were referred to me by someone they met on the beach in San Diego, California. A popular children's magazine finally tracked me down after months of research to request permission to use my poem "AS I GROW" for a promotional gift and paid me an unexpected amount of $1,000.

I could go on and tell you many similar stories in which things fell into place for me against all odds. I imagine that if you think about it, you also have some miraculous stories of your own that you may have labeled as lucky or a coincidence. It is a spiritual truth that there are no coincidences. Everything that happens is perfect even when it does not seem to be that way.

If you desire to create abundance in your life of love, health, service opportunities, friends, money, etc., overcome your negative beliefs about having any of the above. Then re-program yourself by thinking and visualizing that you can have what you want and need. Be open to receiving, and watch for the miracles.

Your spiritual essence knows that it is your birthright to have whatever you need, that you have the power to create it, and that you deserve it all!

STEP TWELVE: FAITH

On the pathway to enlightenment, you have faith that there is an unconditionally loving higher source, often referred to as God. You realize that we are all one, and that you and everyone and everything are an extension of God.

As a spiritual being you understand that this all-loving, omnipotent higher power works through you to bring love and light onto the planet. You accept that you are in a cosmic partnership with God, and you feel humble, grateful, and honored to be a conduit of God's love and light.

Because you have faith, you know that everything is in divine order—that there are no accidents or coincidences. You follow your spirit with no hesitation because you trust that God and you are one. There is no separation. There is only cooperation, service, love, and light. All else is an illusion.

You have faith and trust in yourself to live from your spirit, your divine Godself. You realize that your guardian angel and many other angels, also in service to God, are always there to support, protect, and guide you. You have a deep knowing that you are safe and that all you need will be provided for you.

Recently, my faith was tested. For the first time in all the years I have been driving, my car suddenly lost all of its power on a two-lane mountain highway. I managed to pull over somewhat but was still partially on the road. I put my emergency lights on, stood in front of the car, and patiently waited. My thoughts were, "I wonder who God wants me to meet today." I watched a few cars pass by, and then someone made a U-turn and came back to ask me if I needed help. When the driver found out that I was stuck, she offered to push me off the road and take me to a gas station.

In the course of our conversation, I discovered that she was going through a divorce and wanted to seek professional help for herself and her two children but could not afford the fees. Grateful that she helped me out, and also having faith in the perfection of it all, I offered to give her family a free session. She replied, "You don't have to." I replied, "I know, and I want to." I knew that God was serving through me. I also knew all along that I was protected, supported, and guided.

Another example of how God works to serve our needs and wants is when a tourist called me. Stan wanted to make an appointment before he had to leave Sedona. When I asked him how he heard about me, Stan said, "I was visiting some friends and another couple came over. After talking to the wife, Faith, she suggested that I call you. What is amazing is that just yesterday, I was praying for someone to help me clear away some of my negative beliefs."

Another aspect of faith is surrender. As a very active, assertive, determined being, I never thought that I would love the concept of surrender. But I have learned the hard way, that surrendering to my divine will is the source of my true power. When I have faith and surrender to my spirit, to my God-self, only then do I experience divine power; only then is my life flowing easily and effortlessly.

I'll never forget when I was sharing this concept in a workshop and guided the participants through a process to experience surrendering to their spirit. At the end, a macho-looking man came up to me and said, "Thank you for teaching me how powerful surrender is." I looked into his blue, sparkling eyes, smiled, and replied, "Thank you for getting it, and please pass it on to as many people, especially men, as you can."

The most profound example I recall concerning the power of surrender is what happened to Tom. Since I had moved to the Sierra Mountains from the Silicon Valley area in California, I had not seen Tom for over six months. He was an interesting client who spent many hours listening to motivational tapes and reading numerous books on how to get rich quick. He always seemed to be working on some business scheme.

When Tom called me long distance from San Jose he said, "Helene, I am desperate! I have no job, no money, and I'm about to be evicted from my apartment. I'm terrified, and I don't know what else to do." I replied, "Tom, I suggest that you lie down in an open position, with your palms facing up and your legs apart, relax, and say from the bottom of your heart, I surrender! I surrender to my God-self. I have faith that all that I need is coming to me easily and effortlessly.

Tom, willing to try anything, agreed to follow my guidance. The next day he called me again. This time his voice was very excited. In fact, I had to ask him to slow down so that I could understand what he was saying. Tom had a difficult time containing himself, but he managed to say, "Helene, it worked! This morning I received a call from a big company and they want me to start working for them immediately. After I told my landlord, he said I could stay in my apartment. I am so grateful! Thank you! Thank you! Thank you!" I replied, "Tom that is wonderful. You have succeeded in surrendering to spirit, to faith. Now you are in your true power. You have seen the light, the way, the truth. Congratulations!"

TWELVE-STEPS EXERCISE

Now that we have explored twelve steps to enlightenment, it would be valuable to discover where you are and what your next step is on your spiritual path. The following exercise will help you receive clarity, insights, and solutions. Decide beforehand which one of the twelve steps you are choosing to work with. We will use spiritual relationships as our example.

I have a favorite saying, "Close your eyes and see clearly." When your eyes are closed you can turn inward and see your truth. Find a comfortable, quiet, safe place where you can relax and where you will not be disturbed. Close your eyes and take at least three slow, deep breaths. Imagine that you are visualizing or sensing a stairway with twelve steps in front of you. Now ask yourself, "What step am I on concerning spiritual relationships?"

Then see, hear, sense, or just have a knowing of which of the twelve steps you are on. Now ask yourself, "What can I do now in order to move to the next step in spiritual relationships?" Then visualize or sense yourself doing what you need to do in order to go to the next level in your spiritual growth. Take a few more deep breaths and slowly open your eyes.

Always accept where you are, and value the wisdom you receive. You have all the answers inside of you. It is helpful to write down what you have just experienced and work out the details as to how you will specifically move on to your next step.

You may want to keep a journal or notebook and call it "My Pathway to Enlightenment Workbook." To accelerate your journey, you can repeat the above exercise with each of the twelve steps. Write down the dates, keep notes, take action on your solutions, and watch yourself "fly." Notice how much more you are living in love, joy, and peace.

You can share this simple exercise with others and even organize an enlightenment support group. Make it fun and enjoy the journey.

ENLIGHTENING AFFIRMATIONS

In order to release our self-defeating negative beliefs and to live more in our positive, spiritual part, it is important to pay attention to our daily thoughts and conversations. Whenever you are aware of a negative thought, delete it, and then change it to a positive thought, an affirmation.

It is also helpful to complete each exercise or healing process you do with an affirmation. The more you say, write, read, or sing the new positive thought, the more the belief will integrate into your everyday thinking, and the better you will feel.

The following affirmations can specifically help you to confirm the twelve steps to enlightenment. Notice that they are all positive and written in the present form. If you have difficulty saying any one, you can change it to, "I, (name), and am beginning to believe that I am ___." You can also change the words to fit your needs.

1. I, (name), am living my life from my spirit, from love and joy.
2. I, (name), am listening to and following my intuition.
3. I, (name), am meditating daily to quiet my mind.
4. I, (name), am releasing all my negative thoughts and changing them to positive ones.

88

5. I, (name), am dealing with all my emotions in constructive ways.

6. I, (name), am taking care of my body and honoring it as the temple of my soul.

7. I, (name), am balancing my life between work and play.

8. I, (name), am allowing the abundant, peaceful energy from the universe to flow through me with each breath that I take.

9. I, (name), love myself and others unconditionally.

10. I, (name), am honored to serve others and myself with love.

11. I, (name), am open to receiving an abundance of all that I need and desire.

12. I, (name), am surrendering to my faith in myself and an unconditionally loving higher source.

THE TRUTH IS

The Truth is that enlightenment is our natural state. We are already loving, light-filled beings. On our pathway to enlightenment we are actually peeling away and letting go of all of our illusions, all of our negative thinking and limitations.

The truth is that we have been in denial of whom and what we really are. Now is the time to awaken, to turn the light on, and actualize our spiritual state of being. Now is the time to live in the reality of peace, ease, and grace.

The truth is that we are here on Planet Earth to transcend negative thinking, to live an unlimited life of love and joy, and to feel happy, free, and peacefully powerful.

From this moment on, set your intent to make every day the first day of the rest of your life. Look at the past to learn from it, peek at the future to set up your destination, and live in the present moment. Appreciate and be grateful for all you have, do, and are.

Focus each day not on what you can accomplish, but on how much you can be kind and loving to yourself and others. Forgive everyone, including yourself, and be patient and persevering.

See everyone as your brother or sister, as we are all one global family— all beautiful children of Father God and Mother Goddess.

The truth is we are all light; we are all one!

15: *Knowledge Versus Wisdom*

Are you aware that there is a big difference between knowledge and wisdom? Believe it or not, this information can transform your life. It definitely has affected my life in many profound ways.

Simply stated, knowledge is learned information stored in our wonderful minds. (Intelligence is our ability to learn.) The mind is logical and programmable and in our left brain. The dictionary says it is, "understanding based on experience." It is like a limited computer, because it only knows what you programmed into it. It does not originate new information, but it is great for recording it and passing it on to others.

In contrast, wisdom comes from our spirit. It is non-programmable and it stems from our right brain. Unlike knowledge, it is not learned. Wisdom is intuitive information that is unlimited. We receive the messages from our inner knowing, vision, and words, and/or a gut-feeling. All creativity comes from our intuition. That is where original art, music, inventions, solutions, etc. originate from.

We all have inner wisdom expressed through one or more of the four ways of receiving intuitive messages mentioned above. It goes beyond logic and beyond the physical, and that is why it is called metaphysical. If we only believe what we see with our physical eyes or ears, we are using our knowledge, but not our higher wisdom.

Many years ago, I set my intent to make decisions from my wisdom instead of my logical mind. I have had many wonderful experiences that continue to confirm that I made the right choice.

An example of listening to my inner, wise voice is the time I was driving to a county fair. My friend, Ted, told me that I had better take the parking space that was eight blocks from the entrance because I would not get anything closer. Logically, I could not argue with him. However, my intuition told me to keep going and make a left turn by the entrance. Ted was amazed when a car immediately pulled out and made room for me. I easily find many parking places with my unlimited wisdom. Have you had a similar experience?

Another example of the value of intuition is when I gave a personality-type test to help an eye doctor, John, receive more information about his compatibility with a potential associate doctor, Jeff. After they answered the questions, I met with them to discuss the results. According to this very well-known, logical, accurate personality-test, the two doctors showed good compatibility. They balanced each other's strengths and were likely to co-create a successful partnership.

However, I informed the two doctors that I intuitively felt that Jeff would not stay long. They decided to proceed with the new partnership. They worked well together for a few years. John was very disappointed when Jeff decided to leave for no logical reason.

Besides time and energy, your wisdom can also save your life. I recall hearing on the news that some people followed their intuition and did not go to work at the Twin Towers in New York City on the morning of September 11, 2001. There are many stories of people who followed their inner voice and did not go on their scheduled trip for any logical reason. When they heard the news of the plane or train crash, they were very grateful that they had listened to their intuition.

You can also own your all-wise, all-knowing wisdom. Take the time to quiet your mind and tune into your intuition. Have the courage to trust your inner messages and act on them. It can keep you safe and save you time, energy, and money. It can help you enjoy an amazing adventure called life.

The information in the next chapters will help you enhance your wisdom, your invaluable intuition.

16: *The Power of Your Intuition*

How do you define power? To me, power is fulfilling my potential and helping others to do the same.

In order to be all that we are, we need to connect with all four parts of ourselves—mental, physical, emotional, and spiritual. In our society, we are encouraged to focus on our minds and bodies. Often, in my opinion, the emotions and spirit are left behind.

When we are also aware of our emotions and spirit, we can be more powerful—be more of who we really are. Why is that? Our spirit, which is all-good, all-knowing, all-wise, and all-loving, speaks to us through our intuition.

To tap into this pure, unlimited part of us, we can listen to our inner wisdom and actualize all of our potential. There are four ways in which we can receive intuitive information. Often people have one or two ways that are the strongest. The four different modes of intuition are: a gut feeling, hearing with our inner ear, seeing with our inner eye, or having a knowing—telepathy. It is information that is not learned, programmed, or experienced with the basic five senses. If we just use our mind and our senses, we are limited to what we have learned and experienced.

To connect with your intuition, you can ask yourself the question, "Is it for my highest good to _____ " and fill in the different options to receive a "yes" or "no" answer. Then have the courage to follow it, even if it is not logical.

You can also receive your divine guidance by paying attention to the center of your chest. If you ask a question and you feel a tightness or constriction in that area, the answer is "no." An expansion indicates a "yes."

Intuition is a wonderful way to manifest what you desire and it can empower you in many ways. To begin with, it gives you information that is unique for you.

For example, some supplements, foods, or forms of exercise may be helpful for many people. However, they may not be right for you at the time. Checking with your intuition will assist you in knowing what is appropriate for you.

Another gift your intuition offers you is creativity. There are people who play musical instruments, draw, or paint without any lessons. They are using their intuition. In fact, many inventions and brilliant solutions to problems have come from people's intuitive messages. As you open to your inner wisdom, your creativity can also expand.

The third reason intuition is empowering is in its ability to protect you. For example, did you ever have a gut feeling that you were in an unsafe place and needed to leave? I have had clients who told me they had a strong feeling not to go someplace or to leave earlier and they did not listen. In retrospect, they regretted their decision. The men and women could have avoided being involved with people who had problems.

A fourth advantage to using your intuition is that it can save you time, energy, and money. A friend told me that she intuitively felt it was time to sell some of their stock. Her logical husband made the decision to keep it because it was doing well. Instead of following her gut feeling, she also held on to it. The stock dropped drastically and they both lost thousands of dollars—a very high price to pay for not following the wisdom and foresight of intuition.

As far as time and energy is concerned, did someone ever invite you to participate in a wonderful project or business that you were interested in, but your intuition told you that it was not appropriate for you or it would not succeed? Ignoring your intuition, you liked the idea and invested time, energy, and possibly money, too? Then your intuition proved right and you were sorry that you did not heed the warning?

I have learned my lesson from these experiences. No matter how great an opportunity appears to be, I am committed to using the power of my intuition to guide me as to where to focus my time, money, and energy.

The fifth value of your intuition I will explain with the following spiritual truth: like attracts like. Therefore, if you are acting on your intuition, which comes from total love and for the good of all, you are likely to receive that positive energy back. However, if your mind decides to do something out of fear and anger, these negative feelings are likely to boomerang back to you.

Your intuitive part would never support you to act out of anger, fear, or revenge. It will always encourage you to be compassionate and forgiving, and will also guide you to take the appropriate actions.

Your intuition can also help you solve problems and be healthier. It is generally believed that stress is a killer—the cause of many diseases. Stress comes from negative thinking, fear, or confusion. It lowers our immune system.

How many times were you stressed because you did not know what decision to make? You weighed all the pros and cons, but as soon as you decided the action you would take, another part of you doubted that you were making the right choice. How many nights were you tossing and turning restlessly in your bed because you were not sure what to do?

With the assistance of your intuition, you can tune into your gut feeling, inner voice, visual picture, or telepathy (pure knowing) and receive a clear answer.

Following your intuition is fun. For example, sometimes I am guided to go to a specific restaurant and I meet someone I was trying to connect with. Other times, I am guided to go to an event and I have a great time. When I talked to a friend, who attended a different event I had also considered, I found out that it was not much fun.

Another way your intuition serves you is to help manifest what you desire. However, I suggest that you ask in a spiritual way, because sometimes our personalities think we want something that may not be appropriate for us. For example, you can set your intent by saying, "If it is for my highest good, I *am open to connecting with my perfect partner* (house, business partner, job, school, etc.)

at the perfect time." Then listen intuitively for places to go and opportunities to follow up, so that you can actualize your goal.

Finally, I will explain the power of your intuition through the well-known saying, "*The truth sets you free!*" Your spirit is who you really are, and through your intuition you can uncover all of your uniqueness and gifts and be truly happy. For example, if you are an artist or singer, I encourage you to actively pursue these gifts.

There are so many ways your intuition can assist you to live in more joy, health, happiness, and success. I could write a book about all the avenues, and I believe you could, too, once you re-own the power of your intuition.

17: *Clearing and Protecting Energy*

Everything is energy. You cannot destroy energy but you can transform it. In my experience, there are only two basic emotions— fear and love. Obviously, love energy feels good and fear energy does not. Another important fact is that like attracts like. Therefore, if we are in fear, we can attract fear-based entities on this earth plane and above. Your protection is love energy, because it will attract loving people and loving non-physical beings to you.

We are all human and going to be in our fear space sometimes. However, we do not have to stay stuck in it. When we get our hands dirty, we wash them. It is extremely important to know how to "wash away the fear" and shift from fear into love. Many more reasons and empowering ways are available in my book, *All You Need Is HART! Create Love, Joy and Abundance—NOW! A Unique Guide to Holistic and Rapid Transformation*.

It is also imperative to clear yourself of any fear energy when you check in with your intuition, in order to receive accurate information. That is because the fears cause blocks in your intuitive clarity. To further understand this concept, imagine a television screen that has static lines across the picture. When you remove the fear energy, the screen is clear.

I always make sure that my clients and I are clear before I begin any sessions, so that we can receive accurate messages. If the clients are not clear and we do the clearing process, they immediately feel lighter and better.

Finally, we can clear hotel rooms, planes, cars, homes, offices, and any space that does not feel good. I suggest that you memorize the basic powerful clearing process so that you can practice it often. It has served me immeasurably in many situations.

Burning the herb sage is a popular way to clear negative energy. However, if there are ghosts present, they are likely to go next door or come back later. If you call in the angels as suggested below, they will remove them from the earth plane and take them home to the light, or where they need to go for their soul growth. More information about ghosts are included in the chapter, "Ghost Busting with Love."

CLEARING AND PROTECTING YOURSELF

To release negative energy and protect yourself, you can do the empowering exercise below. It is helpful to do this whenever you are tuning into your intuition, going to bed, waking up (fears may show up in the dream state), or whenever you feel cloudy or stuck.

1. "I am choosing the light. *I set my intent to clear myself."*

2. "I call on Archangel Michael and the Rescue Angels to come in now and remove all entities in and around me that are not from the light, and take them where they need to go for their soul growth. And so it is!"

3. Then imagine a spiral white light circulating counterclockwise (to the left) from under your feet to over your head.

4. Take three slow, deep breaths.

5. "Only beings of the light are welcome in and around me. I call on Archangel Michael, angels, and guides from the light to protect me."

6. Now visualize a swirl of white light coming from above your head and circulating clockwise (to the right) down to below your feet.

7. Take three slow, deep breaths.

CLEARING AND PROTECTING A PLACE

The following is a process to clear and protect a home, school, office, etc.

1. "I am choosing the light. I set my intent to clear my office."

2. "I call on Archangel Michael and the Rescue Angels to come in now and remove all entities in and around the office that are not from the light and take them where they need to go for their soul growth. And so it is!"

3. Then imagine a spiral white light circulating counterclockwise in the entire space from under the floor to above the ceiling.

4. Take three deep breaths.

5. "Only beings of the light are welcome in and around the office. I call on Archangel Michael, Angels, and guides from the light to protect the office."

6. Now visualize a swirl of white light coming from the universe and circulating clockwise throughout and below the office.

7. Take three slow deep breaths.

OTHER WAYS TO CLEAR AND PROTECT YOURSELF

1. "I am only experiencing my energy." Or, "Only love energy enters and leaves my space." Then imagine a circle of white light around you.

2. If you ever feel scared of entities not from the light, you can say the following Hebrew prayer three to five times. It will protect you from negative forces because of its extremely high vibration. It means Holy, Holy, Holy, Lord God of Hosts. *Kadoish, Kadoish, Kadoish, Adonai, Tsebayoth (Say' by' oath').*

99

Cleansing Yourself of Other People's Energy

If you have taken on other people's energy, you can use these clearing processes.

1. Visualize the person(s) in front of you and think or say, "I send you all your energy back to you and I am receiving all my energy back to me." Then imagine the energy exchange.

2. Set your intent to clear your aura. Now imagine a spiral white light flowing counterclockwise all around your aura. Or, imagine that a rose is cleansing your aura (space around your body). When it looks dark, release it to the universe to be re-energized and continue cleansing with another rose.

3. Imagine that the top of your head is opening up and white (or golden) light is flowing from the universe into your body. It is cleansing your body by pushing all negative energy down through your feet and back into the earth to be re-energized.

4. Drop a grounding cord deep into the center of the earth and connect it to the earth. Imagine that other people's energy are flowing down the grounding cord, into the earth to be re-energized.

5. Set your intent to clear your aura. Use your hands to sweep away other people's energy.

Grounding Process

When you are grounded, you are more centered and in control of yourself. This is a good process to do when you awaken and whenever you feel spacey.

1. Allow yourself to drop a grounding cord from the base of your spine down to the center of the earth.

2. Notice that there is a plate there with your name on it. Connect the cord to your plate.

3. Now drop a grounding cord down into the earth from the center of each foot (foot chakras) and attach them to two other plates with your name on them.

4. Take two deep breaths.

5. To further ground yourself, hug a tree or eat something that grows in the earth.

HOW TO PULL PSYCHIC CORDS

Psychic cords that look like ropes or umbilical cords become attached to us when we are afraid or worried about someone, or believe that we need the other person for survival or they need us. They can keep both people stuck in fear and pain. Therefore, they are unhealthy connections and it serves us to cut them, even with those who are deceased.

The only healthy connection is visualizing the pink light of love flowing down from the universe through the top of your head and into your heart chakra (center of your chest) and then to the other person's heart chakra unconditionally. It is up to them whether they are willing to receive it.

Cutting unhealthy cords is a simple, powerful process. You can repeat the exercise with anyone and send loving compassion to them. This empowering process can really make a major difference in your life.

1. Close your eyes and allow yourself to visualize or imagine your mother (father, lover, etc.) in front of you. Notice if there are any cords attaching you to them. How many are you seeing? What do they look like? Where are they attached? (They can be any place on the body.)

2. If you are you willing to cut the psychic cords, then say, *"Mom, I love you and I don't need you for survival and you don't need me for survival. We are here to be our unique selves. Good-bye Mom, Hello (name). I don't need a mother, I need a friend."*

3. Now imagine a scissor or knife cutting the cords.

4. If you cannot or won't cut the cords, then ask yourself, "What are you getting out of the attachment? What do you imagine

would happen if you cut the cords?" Then resolve the issue and remove the cords.

5. When the cords are eliminated, imagine a healing color is coming into your body where the cords were attached. How do you feel?

6. Now imagine the pink light of love flowing down from the universe through the top of your head and into your heart chakra (center of your chest) and then to the other person's heart chakra unconditionally. Continue to send them healing love energy whenever you think of them.

7. Finally, visualize or imagine how your life will be different in a positive way.

SUMMARY OF CLEARING AND PROTECTING ENERGY

Everything is energy. Energy can be moved and transformed but not destroyed. There are only two basic emotions—love and fear. All other emotions are forms of these two. Love is more powerful than fear. There is a universal law that like attracts like. Therefore, if you are in your love space, you are protected from fear energy.

When you are in a loving space, you will only attract love-based beings in body form or entities (beings not in human form). If you are in fear (anger, hurt, guilt, resentment, sad, disappointed, etc.), you are likely to attract fear-based entities that mirror and reinforce your fears.

Fears and fear-based entities cause interference for clear intuition. To understand that imagine that your television screen is filled with lines and you cannot tune-in to a clear picture. In order to receive clear guidance from your intuition, it is important to resolve your fear and remove fear- based entities.

You now have information about how to clear and protect yourself. You can feel empowered and enjoy more love and peace in your life.

18: *Channeling—*
An Ecstatic Experience

Joyful tears were tickling my cheeks as I felt my guide's energy inside of me. I'll never forget the first time I experienced tingling and incredible warm, loving energy flowing throughout my entire body. Any trace of illusion that I was alone on this planet was dissolved. Any doubts of the love, support, and guidance I was receiving from God and spirit guides dissipated. My level of faith took a quantum leap. I KNEW they were there!

Needless to say, I was excited to share this experience with others. I wanted to help people raise their level of faith and feel the fantastic love connection with the cosmos. Since then I have facilitated many clients and workshop participants in meeting and, if appropriate, channeling their spirit guides. They often encountered very powerful spiritual happenings.

Elizabeth described her experience as uplifting and freeing. She felt very light and free of the confines of gravity—free to levitate if she wanted to. Tina said her heart was pounding as she experienced a sparkling energy field that felt like sparks of electricity. Sandy saw colors that she couldn't describe because they were not of this planet. She said, "Now I know what paradise must be like."

Jan experienced a sense of joy and lightness. She found herself in an open heart space—feeling connected to all people. She was aware of transcending her human problems. In fact, everything seemed so simple, clear, direct, fun, and effortless. Jan found herself wondering how we make life so hard and heavy, because from the cosmic prospective, everything looks so easy. She finds channeling exciting and energizing as well as an experience of peaceful power and overall well-beingness.

Bill felt euphoric when he saw his Indian Guide. He said, "It was the same high experience I had when I was drinking." Mark felt his high from channeling was better than when he was on heroin and cocaine. "It was a clear, beautiful high without the side effects. I saw a multi-faceted crystal filled with colors. I couldn't believe the incredible vibrations I felt from the colors. What an experience!"

Joy shared that she also had explored drugs and alcohol, and she was ecstatic about the free, natural high she experienced when she contacted her guides. "I love to channel because no matter how much I'm caught up in my human drama, I always come back to my God-space. And I know that God and I are one!"

These are just a few examples of the many transformational and intensely loving experiences that people encountered as they connected with their spirit guides. I'm delighted to share the art of channeling with you, so that you, too, may have fun and profound cosmic connections, raise your level of faith, and feel the love and support from our divine brothers and sisters of our universal family.

Before you are guided through the channeling process, it is important to have an understanding about guides and the cosmos. The following commonly asked questions and answers will give you the basic necessary information.

WHAT IS INTUITION?

It is a very important, wise, and protective part of you. There are four ways to receive intuitive messages. They are: clairsentience—a gut feeling; clairaudience—something you hear; clairvoyance—images you see in your mind's eye; and telepathy—pure knowing. They are all valid, and you may have developed any or all four ways to intuit. Everyone is naturally intuitive. It is a matter of listening and trusting your sixth sense.

The logical mind has a hard time with this concept because it has limitations and needs physical proof, whereas your intuition is metaphysical, meaning above the physical. When people have trouble with metaphysics, I ask them if they believe in radio waves. When they say "Of course," I remind them that they cannot see the sound waves or feel them on the physical plain. Therefore, they are metaphysical.

There are three levels of consciousness. The subconscious, or "basement," contains our fears, memories, etc. Our conscious, or "first floor," is what we are aware of with our five senses on this physical earth plane. The high conscious, the "attic," is our unlimited spiritual part, also known as our sixth sense or higher self, which is tuned into the universe. The intuitive, metaphysical messages we receive can be from our higher self, or they can be from angels and guides that communicate to us through our higher self.

ARE THERE DIFFERENT WAYS TO CHANNEL?

There are two forms of channeling. In conscious channeling, you remain in your body as the guides join you inside and speak through you. You feel their presence, and you can even speak to them from inside. Often, you will remember most of what occurred. This is the process that you will experience in this book.

In trance channeling, the person actually leaves their body (astral travels) and goes somewhere in the cosmos to study, rest, or heal, and to experience serenity and oneness with the universe. Since they are not present or conscious, they have no memory of the channeling experience. If you have read about, seen, or heard Lazarus or Bartholomew, you have experienced an example of trance channeling. In each case, the person who channels them agrees to leave their body and offer their guide an opportunity to serve people on Planet Earth by taking temporary residence in their physical body.

Is there a difference between meeting your guides and conscious channeling? Yes. You will be guided to travel up to the universe to meet your spirit guides. You may just talk to them and have a delightful time. Then if you feel ready, you may invite their energy into your body and experience their loving vibrations as they speak through you. Meeting your guides and bringing them into your body, which I refer to as conscious channeling, are both valid channeling experiences.

HOW DOES INTUITION FIT INTO ALL THIS?

Intuition, meeting your guides, and conscious channeling are all wonderful ways to connect with your inner wisdom and the love and support of spirit guides. The difference is that with intuition you are not sure who is supplying the information. When you meet your higher self or spirit guide, you find out who is on the other end of the line, who is communicating their love and wisdom.

CAN ANYONE CHANNEL?

I believe that anyone can channel if they desire to and have overcome their fears.

WHAT ARE THE MOST COMMON FEARS THAT NEED TO BE RESOLVED?

I have found that the resistance to channeling is mostly a result of not feeling worthy. The truth is that your higher self and spirit guides from the light never judge you no matter what you think you have done. You are worthy!

Another common concern is that of losing control. Actually, you are in control of whatever happens. It is your choice to surrender to your guide's spiritual energy, as it is to surrender to the water as you jump into the lake. Thank your logical mind for caring and trying to protect you. Reassure it that you are safe.

A third reason people often won't allow themselves to channel is because they have fears of success. Deep down we have a knowing that the experience will empower us, and many people are afraid to be their powerful selves.

I helped many individuals release their past life memories of when they were healers, psychic or spiritual, and they misused their power or were killed or tortured for their abilities. Numerous clients recalled being burned at the stake as a "witch." Many others saw what happened to Jesus and were terrified to walk the spiritual path. The truth is that happened almost two thousand years ago—things are different. It is time to come out now and be who you really are. It is safe!

Some people are afraid to channel because they believe that they are giving others their power and that can be dangerous. I teach people to always keep their power by trusting, above all, their own feelings—what they feel in their heart to be true. Therefore, whether you are listening to a powerful speaker, a therapist, or a spiritual guide, you don't want to automatically take what they say as the gospel truth. Tune into your intuition or heart to find out if what they are saying is a truth for you, to know whom to trust, and practice discernment.

Channeling, like anything else, can be a fantastic experience if you know what you are doing, and can be less desirous if you don't. Like driving a car, it can take you on wonderful journeys but can be dangerous if you do not know how to drive. Skiers who learn how to glide on water or snow can enjoy many blissful moments only if they understand how to ski and take the necessary precautions.

HOW CAN YOU ASSURE YOURSELF OF A POSITIVE CHANNELING EXPERIENCE?

First of all, it is necessary to understand the different dimensions or levels of consciousness. I cannot guarantee the accuracy of the following outline. However, the information that I have received has been helpful as a general guideline. It is important to find out which dimension the guide is from.

I personally recommend that you only channel beings from the fifth dimension or higher. Only then are you sure of receiving pure information, because they are totally in the light and coming from unconditional love. As I channeled entities from the various dimensions, I have felt the differences in the levels of consciousness. Everyone in the room, including myself, experienced more intense love and light from the guides coming from the higher dimensions.

The following are general guidelines of the different dimensions and what is found in each one:

1. One celled animals

2. All other animals

3. Earth: physical bodies and polarities (negative and positive—fear and love)

4. Highly interactive with the third but not in a physical body: fairies, gnomes, elves, ghosts, dark forces, grays (fear-based ETS), polarities (negative and positive)

5. Beginning of total light (no polarities), purely spiritual, heavenly (where you go when you die), angels and spirit guides from the light

6. Basis of language, numerology, astrology, music, and the home of the dolphins

7. Last dimension to be an individual spirit, pure essence exists here

8. Group spirits, spirit of a city or community, and group souls (begin to speak in the "we" form)

9. Entities manifest as planets, stars, galaxies, and universes (earth is a live, conscious group of beings)

10. Beyond, surrounding all dimensions, white light

11. Source of inspiration for the Christ light

12. Twelfth and higher—all one in all universes

(Note: Heaven on Earth is living on the third dimension (Earth) with fifth dimensional or higher consciousness.)

The second important thing to know is that there are confused, Earth-bound spirits who are filled with fear. (Note the Chapter: "Ghost Busting with Love.") The ghosts you hear about in buildings are those stuck entities who are no longer in the physical realm but don't feel worthy enough to go back home to the light where we all come from. Sometimes they are just confused and don't realize they are dead. For obvious reasons, you don't want to channel these spirits.

In my experience, I have also encountered entities known as the dark forces. They are not from this planet and their consciousness is 100% fear. Since like attracts like, these entities are drawn to people who are in fear. Their intent is to keep you in the darkness, and, of course, they do not want you to connect with your light guides and be empowered. The dark forces are not to be feared but to be looked upon as mirrors of our fears, our darkness. (Fear is underneath anger, greed, judgments, depression, etc.)

It is normal and human to experience fears on this planet. Our biggest job here is to become aware of and release these negative, limiting thoughts and feelings so that we can move on in our spiritual growth and live a very happy, healthy, and fulfilling life.

As part of the preparation for channeling, I will guide you through a general clearing process so that you can be free to meet your spiritual guide.

WHAT ARE SPIRIT GUIDES FROM THE LIGHT?

All spirits carry a specific energy that is expressed in a color vibration. Therefore you will be guided to ask the color of their energy to make sure that they are from the light. Bright rainbow colors, silver, gold, and white are the typical color vibrations of the higher guides.

Spirits from the light will come to you in the image of a color, or they will take on a body form to make it easier for you to relate to them. However they choose to appear, they will always look beautiful and feel wonderful.

Higher guides will not deceive you. They will tell you their name and speak to you with total love, acceptance, and patience. Their eyes will be clear and bright. Trust that the perfect guides will come to you at the perfect time. Sometimes you will meet a guide who has been with you in past lives or someone you were a spirit guide for during their incarnation on earth.

Other times, the guide will be a "specialist" in the specific work you are doing. For example, my chosen work is to help people to feel empowered, to heal and love themselves. Therefore, the guides who come to me are also working with the same focus, and they assist me in my service. An artist or musician will attract a spirit with that expertise.

Some of the names of spirit guides that others and I have channeled are: St. Germaine, Archangel Michael, Bartholomew, Jesus, Mother Mary, Isis, Gabriel, Sebastian, Athena, Kwan Yin, Guardian Angel Samantha, The Group of 12, Tom, and George.

IS IT POSSIBLE TO CHANNEL SPACE BEINGS?

It is possible to channel space beings and the same guidelines need to be followed. Some of them, like the Arcturians, are from the 5th dimension and here to serve us—help us back to the light. Other space beings with consciousness from below the fifth dimension are not always helpful.

WHY DO SPIRITS WANT TO HELP US?

Spirits from the light are very humble and grateful for the opportunity to help us because they live in a love vibration and love us dearly. They are very clear that we are one big cosmic family. Also, when they serve us, they are raising their vibrations and moving up to higher levels of consciousness.

The guides need our third dimensional bodies, minds, and technology to ground their service on earth. For example, Bartholomew serves through Mary-Margaret Moore who channels him, and brings his great love and wisdom to many people through his spoken words. Then his divine ideas are transcribed into a book. What a wonderful way Bartholomew, a spiritual guide, has found to serve millions of individuals. Meanwhile Mary-Margaret fulfills her agreement (which she probably made with Bartholomew before she incarnated) to serve in this way and benefits by receiving some "points" to help her raise her consciousness, to help her evolve spiritually.

Guides are always there for us. All we have to do is "pick up the receiver," or "tune into the cosmic station." Working with your loving guides is definitely a win-win-win experience. That is, the guides benefit, as well as you and society.

HOW CAN I PREPARE FOR CHANNELING?

I recommend the following steps to prepare yourself for the channeling experience:

1. **Additional information:** If you have any other questions, read more about the subject or ask a reliable, experienced channel to fill in the missing pieces.

2. **Classes and mentors:** For your first channeling experience, it is a good idea to take a class, or workshop, or have a private session with a qualified person. Let your intuition and feelings guide you to your perfect teacher.

3. **Alone or with others:** Once you have had a good experience with channeling and you feel confident, you can do it in the presence of people you trust or by yourself.

4. **Questions for your guide:** It is a good idea for you and your guests to write down any questions you all want to ask your guide. As you are channeling, your guest can ask the questions and write down the answers. If you are alone, a tape recorder may be helpful to record your experience.

5. **Your environment:** Choose a nice, quiet environment, and find a comfortable place to sit. Peaceful, instrumental music can help you relax and surrender to the experience.

6. **Clearing:** You may want to light a candle and burn sage near and around you to clear the energy. To make sure that you

are clear, say, **"I am choosing the light. Lord Michael and the Rescue Angels, come in now and remove all entities not of the light from myself, others, and the room, and take them to the light or where they need to go for their soul growth. And so it is!"**

Then visualize a swirl of white light coming from the ground and circulating around until you see (or sense) the entire room filled with the light. To further clear the area, ask Archangel Michael, angels, and guides from the light to be in the room for support and protection.

If you become frightened of beings not of the light, say the following Hebrew prayer three times which will protect you from negative forces because of its high vibration. It is: **Kadoish, Kadoish, Kadoish, Adonai, Tsebayoth** *(Say' by' oath')*. The translation is: **Holy, Holy, Holy, Lord God of Hosts.**

7. **Overcoming resistance:** You may find it helpful to say out loud the following positive thoughts or affirmations:

   a) I forgive myself for everything I judged as wrong.

   b) I deserve to connect with guides from the light.

   c) I am ready and worthy of meeting my highest guide from the   light.

   d) I understand that I am always in control.

   e) I trust myself to know who to trust.

   f) I will only use my power for the good of all.

   g) I believe that it is safe now for me to be my powerful self.

   h) I surrender to the experience of channeling a spirit from the light.

8. **What to expect:** Relax and trust that whatever happens is perfect! Like anything else, the more you do it the better you will become at allowing yourself to channel beings from the light.

To be sure that you are channeling a guide from the light, I will take you through five tests. If the guide does not pass any one test of being from the light, then simply use your free will and tell the entity, "I release you into the Universe," and watch it leave. Then say again, "I'm ready to meet my highest guide from the light." Repeat all the tests from the beginning with the new guide that appears. I recommend that you speak to and channel only guides that pass all five of the following tests:

1. Tune into your intuition to decipher if the entity is from the light.

2. Ask the guide, "Are you from the light?" and hear or sense an answer.

3. Ask the guide, "What dimension are you from?" and hear or sense a number. Light beings are from the fifth dimension or higher.

4. Ask, "What is your name?" and hear or sense a name. If you don't understand the name, then ask them to spell it for you. Guides from the light will give you their name and it will sound light.

Ask, "What is the color of your vibration?" and sense or see a color. Only bright colors of the rainbow, silver, gold, and white are light vibrations.

Now we are ready for the channeling process. You can ask someone to read the process to you or record the words on a tape. Remember to leave enough time for you to visualize or sense the experience.

I. RELAXATION PROCESS

Close your eyes. Take two deep breaths.

Now be aware of your body and notice if you have any tension anywhere. If you do, tell that part to relax.

And now imagine a place where you feel safe. It could be a beach, forest, meadow, mountain top, or your own bedroom or living room. Imagine any place where you feel safe and be there now.

Where are you? What are you seeing? What are you hearing? How are you feeling? If there was a color that represented calmness and safety to you what color would that be? Imagine that color is coming into your lungs as you inhale and flowing throughout your entire body, bringing you a deeper level of calmness and safety.

Know that whenever you feel frightened, you can return to your special place, breathe in your calming color, and feel safe again.

Take two deep breaths.

II. MEETING YOUR GUIDE

Imagine that it is evening time and you are looking up at the beautiful, sparkling stars. One of the stars is dropping down from the sky and entering the center of your forehead (your third eye) and filling you with light.

Now allow yourself to float up to the universe as a light body and see a beautiful white door. And say, as you open the door, "I am worthy and ready to meet my highest guide from the light." Now allow yourself to see your highest guide coming towards you. What are you seeing or sensing?

III. THE FIVE TESTS

Do you trust this guide is from the light? (If you don't, tell it to leave and ask for another guide from the light to come to you.)

Now ask the guide, "Are you from the light?" and hear or sense an answer.

If you are convinced that it is from the light, then ask, "What dimension are you from?" and hear a number. Only if the guide is from the fifth dimension or higher, ask it, "What is your name?" and hear or sense a name. If you don't understand the name, then ask the guide to spell it for you.

114

If you feel satisfied with the name, then ask, "What color is your energy?" (If their color is bright and that of the rainbow colors, white, gold, or silver, they are from the light.)   At this point, if you are convinced that your guide is from the light, you may ask the spirit questions and hear or sense the answers.

IV. CONSCIOUS CHANNELING

If you want to bring the guide's vibrations into your body and consciously channel, then ask your guide, "Is it appropriate now for me to bring your energy into my body?" If the guide and you agree that you are ready to channel its energy, then invite the color of its vibration close to your body. If it feels good, then allow it to flow into your body through the back of your neck. Remember that you are remaining in your body and the guide is joining you.

You may find yourself dropping your head to your chest and feeling warm or hot, heavy and/or tingling sensations. These are normal reactions to high vibration energy.

When the guide is fully inside of you, your head is likely to rise if it has dropped, and the guide may say something like, "Greetings, I am _____ (their name)." At that point, it is appropriate for anyone to speak to the guide as you would any other person of wisdom, with respect and gratitude.

V. RELEASING YOUR GUIDE BACK TO THE UNIVERSE

If at any time you begin to feel tired, then tell your guide and he/she (actually they are androgynous) will bid farewell. They often know they must leave before you realize that it is time for them to go. They don't want to tax your energy.

Allow the guide's energy, in the form of their color vibration, to leave through the back of your neck and return to the Universe, and see the door closing behind it. (Your head may drop again.) Now imagine that you are back on the mountain top and looking up at the stars. Slowly but surely, become aware of your body—move your fingers and toes. Then drop a grounding cord from the bottom of your spine and from the center of the bottom of both feet deep into the Earth. Imagine that you are connecting the three grounding cords in some way to the center of the Earth.

Take a few deep breaths, and slowly open your eyes. If you still feel spacey, rest awhile and/or eat something grown in the earth and drink some water.

Congratulate yourself for surrendering to a spiritual experience. Once you have your guides' names, and you have many, you can talk to them anytime, anywhere, and anyplace. They are always there for you. Feel free to call on them and enjoy a divine interaction filled with love, support, and wisdom.

People are often surprised when they realize that many individuals channel the same spirits. The guides are evolved and are capable of being in many places at the same time.

You may find that one guide will come to you for a while, and then another will appear. Ask them why they came to you. There is always a logical answer.

For example, one day I was surprised to meet the Indian Guru Sai Baba behind the door. When I asked him what message he had for me, he told me I was too Western and needed to be more Eastern to be in better balance. It was important for me to take the time to just be quiet, relax, meditate, and enjoy nature. I was very grateful for this timely guidance. As usual, it was perfect! Since I acted on the message, he hasn't appeared again.

I find it fun, profound, and very rewarding to meet my guides almost daily. They serve me in different ways, but the answer I receive from my question, "What should I do now?" is always, "Dear one, be in peace."

19: *Ghost Busting with Love*

Are there unexplained sounds or peculiar things happening in your home? Are you aware of heavy or negative energy in specific areas of your environment? Do you notice that there are certain places that you avoid going to for no logical reason?

If you relate to any of these situations, it is possible that you have encountered spirits, otherwise known as ghosts. I myself was very skeptical of that concept until I personally became aware of spirits and learned how to be what I call "a loving ghost buster." Here are some fascinating experiences I have had where everyone benefited—friends and spirits.

One Friday evening in my home in the gold country, I was lying face down on a massage table and talking to Joy, the massage therapist who knew that I helped release spirits. I said, "Joy, I found it very difficult to be in your house last week, especially in the living room. I think it would be a good idea to check and see if there are any ghosts hanging around."

Joy, also a very sensitive, intuitive person, acknowledged that she was aware of "heavy" energy in her home. She seemed pleased when I offered to visit her the following week in order to clear her space.

Once that was settled, I closed my eyes and relaxed so that I could enjoy the therapeutic massage. Much to my surprise, I spontaneously started to see a vivid image of her living room. It was as if a movie had begun to play in my mind.

Four unshaven men wearing worn plaid shirts, with suspenders holding up their mud-stained jeans, were sitting around an old card table and laughing about how they had cheated a speculator of his gold. The dusty living room was decorated with a brown rickety couch, a half-broken table, a dully lit lamp, and rusty mining tools. The dirty windows were covered with white stained sheets.

The sound of a crackling fire in the fireplace filled the room. In front of each man was an uneven pile of colored poker chips. The laughing, heavy-set man with a cigar hanging from his lips threw down his winning three aces in the center of the table and was grabbing the pot when the door suddenly burst open. Entering the room without a word, a tall, thin, dark-haired man with revenge burning in his eyes sprayed bullets into the four miners. Emotionless, satisfied that his mission was accomplished, the killer turned around and walked out, closing the door behind him. Except for the crackling of the fire, there was dead silence in the room.

In my mind, I silently asked the miners, "Why didn't you all go to the light?" The obese miner replied, "I didn't feel worthy because I was so greedy." I reassured him and the other miners that God never judges you, that He loves you unconditionally. I told them lovingly that they were all worthy of God's love; they were worthy of going to the light.

Then I called on the rescue angels to come in and take these four spirits to the light. I noticed that the gruff face of the heavy-set man turned soft and teary-eyed as he and the others left with the angels. They looked so relieved to go "home" to the light. After they left, the living room was filled with bright light.

This clearing of spirits took a few minutes, and I felt honored. I felt as though God was working through me to help these stuck souls, his lost children, who were under the illusion that they were unworthy to go home.

When it was all over, I said, "Joy, the most incredible thing just happened." Joy was excited to hear all about my experience, and she left that evening with great anticipation, wondering if she would feel any changes in her home.

The next day, Joy called to report how much better the living room felt. She also told me that her roommate, Pat, who was unaware of what had transpired, noticed the difference, too. Pat said, "When I woke up during the night and put the light on in the living room, it seemed unusually bright." I was pleased to hear the confirmation that what had happened had really made a difference in their home.

The following Monday evening, I shared this exciting event with my friend Judy when I visited her in the San Francisco Bay Area. Judy's eyes opened wide as she related to me that she and her roommate, Sue, always locked their bedroom doors at night, even though they basically felt safe in their exclusive neighborhood. They both heard many strange, unexplainable noises coming from the attic and the stairs.

Judy asked me if I could help her find out what was happening in her house. I suggested to her that she close her eyes and relax, and then guided her to explore her attic. She had a look of surprise on her face as she said, "No wonder I've been hearing so much noise. I see four Indians living up there."

When Judy asked the Indians why they did not go to the light, they replied, "We didn't feel worthy of the Great Spirit." They went on to explain that while they were away on a hunting trip, their tribe was attacked and all their people were killed. These Indians were convinced that they had disgraced their tribe because they lived and did not die in honor with the others.

At that point, I suggested to Judy that she say to the Indians, "Someone who loves you is coming to take you home to the light. Who do you see or sense?" The Indians were amazed to see their grandfather, who they had thought was angry with them. Judy was touched as she noticed the look of overwhelming relief on the Indians' faces as their grandfather reached out his hands to them, smiled, and said, "I want you to come home with me." Finally convinced that they were worthy of going to the light, the Indians took the hands of their beloved grandfather, who was also their great spiritual leader, and together they all floated up to the light.

The attic seemed to be clear, so we went downstairs to the living room. Judy visualized a scared little boy who looked Mexican standing behind the drapes. She noticed that he was wearing white natural cotton pants and top, and sandals.

At first, the frightened little boy would not speak to us. However, when he was convinced that we wanted to help him, that we would not hurt him, he told us his story. His name was Pedro. When the uncle who had been taking care of him died, Pedro was brought to live in a house on this property. He was treated like a slave and abused in many ways, including sexually. He felt guilty because of the sexual abuse. When he died, he decided that he was unworthy of the light. Pedro felt safe in Judy's house, and was adamant about staying. However, when we called someone who loved him to come down from the light, his uncle appeared. Both Judy and I felt such joy when little Pedro smiled, grabbed his uncle's hand, and disappeared into the light.

The next person we noticed was a woman sitting on the couch. She told us that her name was Millie, and that she had married against her parents' wishes. Her husband had died soon after their wedding. Devastated and alone, Millie could not return to her family because she had left home without permission. She died soon after of a broken heart but stayed in her house for fifty years. When Judy had bought the used couch, Millie had come with it.

During the release process, Millie's husband came to take her back to the light. She was hesitant to go with him, however, because he had left her before. After she heard him tell her how sorry he was to leave her and how much he loved her, Millie gave in and left happily in his arms.

In the kitchen, we found another entity named Michael in his wedding clothes. He had been on the way to his wedding when he was killed in a car accident. Michael still seemed stunned as he said, "I'm looking for my fiancée. I'm not leaving. I have to find her."

I asked the universe to help us find Michael's fiancée. When Cathy appeared, we discovered that she was also deceased and stuck on earth because she would not leave without Michael. Cathy was wandering around searching for her beloved. It was wonderful to be able to help reunite the loving couple. All of us had tears of joy when wedding guests came down to earth to take Michael and Cathy to the light.

Finally, Judy's house was clear of entities, and we went to sleep feeling a great sense of satisfaction.

During breakfast the next morning, Judy asked her roommate, Sue, who did not know what had happened the evening before, if she noticed anything different during the night. At first, Sue had nothing to report. Then after a few minutes she said, "Come to think of it, it was the first night that I did not lock my bedroom door."

A month later, Judy called to tell me that she was awakened during the night by noises coming from her bedroom closet. When she was getting dressed for work the following morning, she discovered that a part of her closet organizer was broken, and all of her clothes had fallen on the floor. When Judy took the pegs to the store to be fixed, the salesperson expressed her surprise because she had never before seen those parts broken in that way.

Suspicious at this point, Judy tuned into the closet and was aware of a spirit hiding in there. Afraid to deal with it by herself, she called me for help. When I asked Judy to close her eyes and to imagine that she was exploring the closet, she was able to picture a man who said his name was Bill. When she asked Bill why he was in there, he said, "Judy, I have been trying to get your attention. I came looking for you because in a past life we were married, and I told you I would never leave you. I broke that promise when I was accidentally hit by a train and died. I'm so sorry."

Judy recognized Bill's spirit and began to sob. She told me that she did not want to release Bill back to the light because she was lonely, and it felt good to be with her beloved again. I asked Judy to visualize a rope going to the left, to her past lives, and to see a knot on it for every lifetime she had a beautiful, loving relationship with Bill. She saw many knots on the rope.

I helped Judy realize that if she wanted to be with Bill again it would be best to encourage him to go back to the light. Then there was a possibility that he could return to earth again at a time when she would also be here. Judy began to understand that if Bill's spirit is earthbound, he is stuck and there is no possible way he can reincarnate. After Judy grieved her loss of Bill, she was ready to let him go, and she saw his mother coming down to take him home to the light.

If you are encountering spirits, you may want to surround yourself with white light and guide them with these words: "You're worthy of the light. It's time for you to return home so that you can continue with your soul growth. You'll be safe and nurtured there. The light is where you belong. Look up and see someone you love coming from the light to take you home."

Encourage the spirit to go with that loving being only if they totally trust them, only if their eyes are soft and loving, and their outstretched hands are warm. These are indications that they are truly from the light. Keep them in your vision until you see them disappear into the light.

If you are aware of a deceased loved one in your environment, you may want to preface all the above actions with these healing words: "I forgive you for the times I felt hurt by your words or actions. Please forgive me for the times you felt hurt by my words or actions. (Then imagine that they are forgiving you, and forgive yourself.) I love you and I am letting you go."

If you have any problems seeing a loved one come from the light to take the spirits home, call on Archangel Michael and the rescue angels to take the person to the light or wherever they need to go for their soul growth.

 It has been a wonderful experience to be a loving "ghost buster" and help many lost spirits release their fears that they are anything but God's children, and then to help them fly home on the wings of love.

A STUBBORN ENTITY

One day I received an intriguing e-mail on my computer entitled

"Stubborn Entity." It went on to say, "An angry entity that feels hate is inside of me. I tried to release him with the process you wrote in your 'Ghost Busting with Love' article, but he won't leave. Do you have any suggestions?"

The electronic letter was sent from Europe from a man who I will refer to as Jon. I wrote back that I needed to talk to him on the phone to help him release the spirit.

When Jon called at the prearranged time, he seemed nervous and desperate. He had been trying for over two years to get rid of this entity. In fact, Jon told me that when he looked into the mirror, he saw an angry face that wasn't his.

As an experienced therapist, I know that we create our reality, and that there must have been a good reason why Jon's free will did not seem to be honored; the entity must have been serving him in some way.

Therefore, I said, "Jon, when did you become aware of this being?"

Jon related that two years ago he had been on vacation with his friend Paul, and they were arguing a lot. It was shortly after that when he noticed this angry face.

I continued, "How did you feel when you were quarreling with Paul, and what decision did you make?"

The thirty-two-year old man replied, "I felt helpless and powerless, and decided that I was not good enough."

When I asked Jon if Paul reminded him of anyone from his past, he answered, "Yes, my father."

Then I suggested that Jon go back to the time when he had those same helpless and powerless feelings with his father. Jon regressed back to being three years old when his dad was very angry with him and he decided that he wasn't good enough.

After we did a healing process to help Jon release that painful experience—and the decision about himself that arose out of it—he realized that he *was* good enough and felt lighter. I explained to Jon that love is his power, and I encouraged him to forgive his father and beam the pink light of love from his heart to his dad's heart. Jon acknowledged that he did feel more powerful.

The next step was to return to the negative experience he had with his friend Paul and do a similar healing process. It is interesting to note that the attached entity was another angry male, and Jon had the same feelings with him—hopeless and powerless. By now, Jon was feeling a lot better, more relaxed and hopeful.

We were now ready to deal with the entity. I asked Jon to speak to the angry entity in the following way: "What is your name?" Through

Jon, the being answered "Brian." Jon continued, "Thank you for serving me. I now release you into the light. Archangel Michael and rescue angels, please come in now and take Brian back to the light."

Almost immediately, I could see (and Jon could feel) the entity leaving him. It is always a touching experience to facilitate a being's return to the light. With disbelief, Jon asked, "Is it really gone?" I replied, "Look into the mirror and tell me what you see."

"He's not there," exclaimed Jon. "Is he really gone?" I intuitively tuned in and said, "Brian is back in the light." I understood that it might take time for Jon to believe that what just happened had really occurred. After two years, it was quite startling to be free from the angry entity in just fifteen minutes.

I reassured Jon that the entity was gone and asked him to let me know tomorrow what happened.

The next day, he wrote me an e-mail in which he said, "I didn't sense him around anymore, but I can hardly believe he's gone. He was such a burden to me. I understand, however, that he was mirroring my own anger. I also understand that when I met people who behaved like my father, I would feel helpless and powerless, because I was following the patterns I had made when I was very young. Now I can choose to radiate love from my heart, instead of anger. When I am doing this, I won't feel powerless. I can't find the right words to thank you!"

A few days later, I heard from Jon again. He was concerned that the entity fooled us, because he felt a being inside of him. I tuned into Jon and then wrote what I received intuitively. "Dear Jon, Brian is gone but there is another entity there that is mirroring your sadness for all the years you were in so much pain. Those feelings are very common following a major breakthrough. Let me know if you need help clearing the entity."

I was pleased to receive his next message that read, "Thank you for the information. I was able to release the entity myself and I feel a lot better." This time the simple spirit release process worked for Jon because he was clear and able to come from love. He was convinced now that the so called "stubborn entity" was helping him to heal his past.

GHOSTS THAT SERVE US

Jane and her husband, Ray, were struggling with the remodeling of their home. Everything that could go wrong did. Needless to say, they were very frustrated. Jane, a forty-two-year-old petite woman, was extremely psychic. One day she told me that she sensed there were entities in the house. When I tuned in, I discovered an old Indian man under the house. He told us that it was his land and he lived there. He was angry that Jane and her husband had the audacity to have their home on his homeland.

When I helped the Indian realize that he was dead and that it was time to go home to the light and be with his loved ones, he eagerly left. Jane sighed with relief.

A week later, Jane told me that more things were being accomplished in the house, but everything seemed to take an extremely long time. With Jane's permission, I intuitively tuned into her and uncovered another piece to the puzzle. Jane and Ray were having marital difficulties, and they unconsciously wanted the focus to continue to be on the house and not on their relationship, so that they wouldn't have to face their problems.

With this new awareness, Jane and Ray were willing to schedule marriage counseling sessions. It was interesting to note that as they dealt constructively with their problems, some things in the house were finished, and before too much longer, the remodeling was completed.

Notice that the entity under the house was in some way actually serving the couple. I notice this to be a common occurrence.

During one private session, we were exploring why Jane often avoided being physically intimate with her husband. Jane discovered that unconsciously she was angry at men, and it was her way of punishing them. However, even with this new awareness, Jane did not want to heal her issues with men.

I suspected that an entity was reinforcing her negative decision. Sure enough, we discovered an angry woman in her genitals who identified herself as Mary. The ghost told us that she entered Jane three years earlier. Jane then realized that that was the time when she started to lose interest in sex. The truth is that Jane was angry with men, and the ghost just reinforced her feelings. Mary was able to attach to Jane because she had the same fears (like attracts like).

I encouraged Jane to say to the angry entity, "Thank you, Mary, for serving me. I don't need you anymore. I release you now to go home. You are worthy of the light. Someone who loves you is coming down to take you back to the light."

When Mary saw her loving deceased grandmother coming down to help her, she softened and said to Jane, "I'm sorry if I hurt you in any way. Please forgive me." Jane did forgive Mary and then encouraged her to go with her grandmother. When the two of them disappeared into the light, Jane took a deep breath of relief and was ready to release her negative feelings about men. She understood now how the ghost had been serving her.

This case study is typical of what I have experienced with many clients. If someone has resistance to letting go of a negative belief, it may be because there is an entity present. It is then necessary to release the attached being before you can help the individual overcome their own fears.

Another client, Rose, a fifty-three-year-old woman, asked me to help her overcome her depression and weight issues. In one counseling session, Rose talked about a strange experience she had in her home. She was ironing in the spare bedroom and decided to take a lunch break. She stood the iron up and turned it off. To her surprise, when she returned to the room an hour later, the iron was facing down. Rose was puzzled because she was sure that she didn't leave it that way.

"It felt eerie, Helene," Rose explained. "That room was my younger daughter's bedroom. She died six years ago. Could it be that she was trying to tell me something?"

I guided Rose to close her eyes and to go back to that scene in the bedroom. I asked her to look around and let me know if she could visualize her daughter there. Sure enough, Rose and I discovered her daughter, Pam, standing next to the ironing board. I suggested to Rose that she speak directly to her.

The grieving mother cried and cried before she could utter a word. She still felt so badly about her beautiful daughter's death due to an illness. Once she composed herself, she talked to Pam and told her how much she missed her.

Pam explained to her mother that she was okay and very happy. She encouraged Rose to let go of her and allow herself to be happy, too. The loving daughter reassured her mother that she had done all that she could, and that she was not responsible for her death. Pam continued on to tell her bereaved mother that it was her time to go, because she had work to do on the other side.

After Rose heard those loving and comforting words, she felt much better. She was ready to release her daughter. We did not have to do anything to assist Pam, because she was already in the light. Pam just came down to the earth plane to talk to her beloved mother, to console her.

Rose looked very peaceful once she was convinced that her daughter was fine and that she no longer needed to feel guilty about her death. The issue she had just resolved had been a major factor contributing to her depression and weight gain. Rose was "stuffing" her emotional pain and punishing herself for her guilt feelings. These are two common causes of people being overweight.

This is just one example of many situations in which I have been honored to facilitate a healing with deceased loved ones. It is very common for ghosts of parents, grandparents, spouses, siblings, or friends to try to help their loved ones on this plane. I refer to these beings as loving, benevolent ghosts/angels. Sometimes they contact you in your dreams. Other times, they show up when you are awake. Whenever or wherever they appear, talk to them and allow them to assist you. It is a gift for them and for you.

"LUCIFER, ARE YOU FOR REAL?"

It was the Monday morning of Labor Day weekend. As I was leaving the sleep state and entering waking consciousness, I became aware of an intense pain in my face and head. When I tuned into the pain, I saw an image of a scorpion. His black, hairy feet were attached to my right cheek, forehead, and scalp and were causing me a lot of pain. Then I heard the words in my head, "Lucifer does not want you out there! Lucifer does not want you to bring love to the planet."

Scared and miserable, I knew that I needed help. Fortunately, I was able to call a friend who I knew would understand my dilemma. Steve, a professional psychic, confirmed that what I was experiencing was very real. He immediately called his teacher of spirit release, and set up a three-way telephone conference call. Brad reassured me that he had come across this phenomenon numerous times in his work, especially with people like me who were making a difference on the planet.

Luckily, he had left an opening Tuesday morning for an emergency, and I was definitely it. Meanwhile, Brad suggested that I burn some candles and do a ritual for releasing the entities. After I followed his instructions and put ice on my painful spots, most of my discomfort released.

The three-hour session was amazing. After a while, we lost count of all the entities that were in and around me. I was a great target because I had recently come down with Bell's Palsy (temporary paralysis of the right side of my face), and I was in a physical and emotional weakened state. My fear consciousness matched theirs—like attracts like.

Being a psychotherapist, author, and speaker, I was definitely helping many people make the shift from fear to love consciousness—from darkness to light, from Lucifer to God.

But I had many fears of success, mainly because of my experiences in previous lifetimes. As a spiritual leader, I had been tortured or killed for my efforts. Even though I knew I was here to make a difference on the planet, my cellular memories of those horrible outcomes were causing me to sabotage myself (something I also discovered in many of my clients). I therefore realized that my own fears of doing this type of work and serving the planet were drawing the negative entities to me.

The way I understand it, God created all of us, His children, in the image of Himself, which is Love and Light. Then, because God loves His children, He gave us free will. To exercise free will, we need choices. So God asked a light being, Lucifer (also known as the devil), to play the role of the darkness, the fear consciousness (the opposite of love).

Back to the question, "Lucifer, are you for real?" I believe that he is really playing a role in our growth. Lucifer and all his fear-based entity helpers (in some circles known as the dark forces) mirror our darkness, our fear-based beliefs and choices. The problem is that these entities reinforce our negativity. That is why we need to release the entities as well as the fears. Then, when we are choosing love and light, no fear-based entities can enter us, because our energy is incompatible. Our love and light is our protection.

THE FOUR DIFFERENT TYPES OF GHOSTS

There are basically different types of ghosts. The first category I refer to as "uninvited house guests." These beings are just earthbound lost souls hanging around. They won't hurt you and they are easy to assist back to the light.

The second type I call the "attached entity." This ghost has found its way inside of you and is affecting you in some way. However, as in the case of Jon, your energy has to be open to it. As the saying goes, "like attracts like." Your belief system must match theirs. After you release the entity, it is wise to clear yourself of the belief so that you don't attract another.

The third class I refer to as "dark forces." These are beings that are not stuck on earth as the other two types of ghosts. Supposedly, dark forces work for the devil, for Lucifer. (Ironically, Lucifer means the light.) They can hurt you, but remember one of the basic spiritual laws: "There are no victims, only volunteers." On some level, you have been in agreement with these beings. They appear as red or black entities instead of in human form because they are not from this planet.

The fourth class I will call "demonic." Personally, I have not had experiences with them. From what I understand, they are extremely "evil" and strong. If I do come across them, I will use the same loving methods to release them, because I know the universal law that love is my power; love always overcomes "evil." To me, "evil" is fear, and love neutralizes fear. I believe that love is the universal antidote for the poison of fear.

If you ever feel afraid of entities not from the light, you can say the following Hebrew words three times. It will protect you from negative forces because of its high vibration. The prayer is: **Kadoish, Kadoish, Kadoish, Adonai, Tsebayoth** *(Say' by' oath')*, **and it means Holy, Holy, Holy, Lord God of Hosts.**

HOW TO BE A LOVING "GHOST BUSTER"

Many ghosts hang around hospitals, funeral homes, and, of course graveyards. Wherever someone dies, their ghost may stay there until he/ she is helped back to the light. Ghosts can easily enter you when you are under the influence of alcohol or drugs. I believe that many alcoholics and drug addicts have attached entities that reinforce their destructive behaviors.

It is a good idea to protect yourself when you have an operation or walk into a hospital, cemetery, or funeral. One way you can do that is to visualize a white light around you and set your intent by saying something like, "Only beings from the light are welcome in my space," or, "Only love energy enters and leaves my space."

If you want to clear yourself, a home, motel, or any space of ghosts, you can simply say these words: "I am choosing the light. Archangel Michael and rescue angels, come in now and take all entities not from the light that are in or around me to where they need to go for their soul growth. And so it is!" Then visualize a spiral of white light coming from the ground and circulating around you and/or the space and going up to the sky.

I recommend that you do this process regularly. Since like attracts like, if you have some fearful thoughts (welcome to the human race!), then you are open to fear-based entities. I personally do this clearing process at least twice a day—in the morning when I awaken and in the evening before I retire.

Another way to clear ghosts is to burn sage, and as you walk around spreading the smoke say, "I am choosing the light. All entities not from the light are to leave now." If you are clearing yourself, then circle the smoke around your whole body—including under your feet.

It is often suggested that you open the windows or doors with the intention of giving them a way out. Personally, I think that they came in through the walls and they can go out the same way. Do what feels right to you. You can purchase sage in loose form or wrapped in a stick in many metaphysical or health food stores. Many people, including me, love the smell. However, the ghosts hate the odor from sage, and they will probably just move on to another home.

If you feel comfortable helping the ghost out of its painful, stuck place, then you can assist them back to the light. "Ghost Busting with Love" is easy to do and a gift to your neighbors, the entity, and you.

If your pet is acting strange (they are intuitively able to see these entities), or if you hear unexplained noises, feel someone's energy, or intuitively see or sense a ghost, then you can follow the ghost busting process below. There is no need to be frightened of the lost soul. Treat the being as you would anyone else you meet on the street who looks lost and confused. With kindness and compassion, show him/her the way.

To begin with, I suggest that you surround yourself with white light and guide them with these loving words: "Hello. What is your name? I am not going to hurt you. I want to help you. How did you die? You're worthy of the light. It's time for you to return home so that you can be with your loved ones and continue with your soul growth. You'll be safe and nurtured there. The light is where you belong. Look up and see someone who loves you coming down from the light to take you home."

When a loving deceased being appears, ask the ghost: "Who has come to take you home?" After they tell you if it is a relative or friend, then ask, "Do you trust that person? Do their eyes appear loving? Hold on to their outreached hand. Does it feel warm?" These are all signs that the being is from the light.

Meanwhile, check into your intuition to see whether you are convinced that this new being is from the light. If either one of you does not feel good about this being, then say to them, "I release you with love and light," and see them disappear. Then say again, "Someone from the light who loves you is coming to take you home." Encourage the ghost to go with them, only after both you and the lost entity are convinced that the spirit companion is truly from the light. Send them on their way with love and compassion, and keep them in your vision until you see them disappear into the light.

If the ghost resists returning to the light because they have unfinished business, you can say, "You are dead now and you can't do what you want to do on earth. If you go back to the light, however, you can be born again and make a difference."

When the lost entity is scared and afraid of the unknown, you can try the following comforting words: "When you return home, familiar loving beings will help you heal and once again become acclimated to the light. Then, when you are ready, you can incarnate again on Planet Earth or wherever else you choose."

If the being is afraid to go to hell because of his/her behavior, you can reassure him/her in the following way: "There is no hell. Everything you have done was for the learning experience called life. If you feel you need to, forgive yourself now. The Divine Source never judges you. He loves and accepts you unconditionally and always welcomes all his children home with open arms. You are worthy of the light and God's love."

When you are aware of a deceased loved one in your environment, you may want to preface the above guidance with these healing words. "I forgive you for all the times I felt hurt by your words or actions. I'm sorry for all the times I may have been hurtful to you. Please forgive me. I love you and I now let you go."

In situations in which you have difficulty seeing a loved one come from the light to take the spirit home, say, "Archangel Michael and the rescue angels, please come now and take this person to the light or wherever he/ she needs to go for his/her soul growth."

If you don't choose to be the one to release the ghost to the light, then find someone who can. The ghost will be very grateful.

Acknowledge yourself for doing an angelic service. You will probably find "ghost busting" to be a wonderful, loving experience when you realize that you are helping lost spirits release the fear that they are not loved and accepted by God and then helping them fly home on the wings of love.

DEALING WITH DARK FORCES

Dark forces can be more difficult to release. It is advisable to seek professional help, especially if you are dealing with "demonic" beings.
 However, if you desire to release a fear-based entity, then I suggest that you first read the section above, "Lucifer, Are You For Real?" Once you have a better understanding of these beings, then you can prepare by surrounding yourself with white light and setting your intent. "I am choosing the light. Only loving beings from the light may enter my space." Remember to stay in your love space, as love is your power.

Then ask the person who has the attached entity if they are choosing the light. If they are willing to, then ask them to say the words, "I am choosing the light."

Now you can address the entity. "We see you entity. What is your name? You have been under the illusion that you are not of the light. The truth is that we are all God's children, and that you are also from the light. Look inside yourself and see your spark of light." They often sheepishly see their spark of light, as they realize that you are speaking the truth. Then say, "Archangel Michael and the rescue angels, please come in now and take this entity to the light or wherever they need to go for their soul growth."

Meanwhile, ask the person (their eyes are closed) to describe what they are visualizing. They will probably tell you that they see a black or red blob leaving their bodies or their space. Those who don't see anything are likely to say they feel as though something is being lifted away. Since a law of the universe says that wherever there is a void, it will be filled, then guide the person to fill the emptied space with white light.

The process of spirit release can be a very healing and rewarding experience for all concerned. Congratulate yourself for performing a divine service; helping confused, fear-based entities, who are under the illusion that they are separate from God and not from the light, to return home to our Father/Mother—to return home to Love and Light!

20: *My Past-Life Story*

"It Is Not Safe for Me to Be Powerful and Help People"

I was exiled in the desert. I wandered about alone and aimlessly in my torn and dirty garments. The glaring hot sun burned my body and dried my throat. There was no water to quench my screaming thirst. At night the cold desert air mercilessly attacked my unprotected body. I was broken- hearted, hurt, and bitter. Eventually I died of starvation and dehydration.

It happened in the eighteenth century. My Arab husband was one of the men in the group who abandoned me to die in the desert—my punishment for trying to organize the women in protest against the social injustices of the times.

This particular past-life regression was the first time I recalled a decision that still haunts me now, in my present life: "It is not safe for me to be powerful and lead people to freedom."

To my surprise, this past-life experience was only the beginning. In other past lives, I was tortured and sometimes killed for helping people. This experience seemed to be a dominant theme for me in many lifetimes. I was stoned in Russia, burned at the stake in Spain, guillotined in France, and tortured on the rack a number of times.

The past-life regressions helped me understand why I held myself back from totally being who I really am. It is true that I have been doing wonderful service—but I also find myself sabotaging many of my efforts to reach my goals.

It often feels like an internal struggle. A part of me naturally knows how to lead people to freedom and how to help them heal themselves. My soul, the part of me that records everything that has happened in all of my lifetimes, is filled with inner strength, courage, and great insights. However, my soul's memories also keep playing a recording of the "tape" that says, "Don't be too powerful or helpful because you will be hurt or killed."

Can you relate to my situation? Do you sometimes feel that two parts of you are pulling you in opposite directions? I call that particular tug-of-war, the Fear of Success.

Early in my private practice as a Marriage and Family Therapist, I discovered the phenomenon of Fear of Success. I had never heard or read anything about this concept. I found it fascinating that so many of my clients were afraid of achieving the very things they were striving for. I was very excited about this new information, and I lectured extensively on the subject. I also facilitated workshops, made a cassette tape, appeared numerous times on radio and television shows, and wrote my first book, *Free to Fly – Dare to Be a Success.*

Meanwhile, my clients were teaching me another incredible lesson. In the process of guiding them back to the times when they made negative decisions, some of them slipped back into past lives. My intuition told me to work with these previous lifetimes the same way I did with present life experiences. It worked well, and I was totally amazed at the positive results. Issues that were still haunting the clients after months of therapy were successfully resolved when they healed their painful past lives.

In the beginning, when the clients first started to regress back to other lifetimes, I was not even sure that I believed in reincarnation. But being a pragmatic person, I did what seemed to work. The process of taking the clients through their past lives was definitely showing great results. They looked more relaxed after they released the negative thought they had made from the negative past life. In the weeks that followed, they expressed to me how much better they were feeling about themselves and others, and how their lives were improving.

To assist you to create what you want in your life, I will share with you, in the next two chapters, what some of my clients and I learned about how our past lives affect our present decisions. You may find that these experiences relate directly to you, or help you to remember your past lives.

To facilitate your understanding of the case studies and exercises in this book, I will explain the therapeutic process I developed. HART: Holistic and Rapid Transformation (also known as Creative Therapy) is based on my observation that we make decisions based on our experiences, even past- life experiences. These decisions, or beliefs, control our lives.

For example, my experience of being abandoned to die in the desert because of my actions led me to make the decision, "It is not safe for me to lead people to freedom." As a result, I had been unconsciously preventing myself from reaching many of my goals in this lifetime.

Another basic principle of HART is that we are all totally responsible for our lives. In other words, there are no victims, only volunteers. I am not saying that you should feel blame or guilt. What I am expressing is my belief that your soul selected the conditions and circumstances of your present lifetime before you were born in order to learn your chosen lessons. Your soul carries memories of everything that ever happened to you in all of your lifetimes and also remembers all of the decisions you have made. It is the soul part of you that makes you unique.

For instance, I am working hard to reach a desired goal, which is to help many people overcome their emotional obstacles and to feel free as a result of reading this book. If I do not succeed in having this book published, there is a part of me that is responsible. Notice that I did not say I would fail to have it published, because I do not believe that is the case.

In my understanding, we all create everything that happens to us, either consciously or unconsciously. Therefore, if I am not getting the results I want, it is because a part of me is succeeding in holding me back until I learn whatever lesson is appropriate at this time, or until I overcome the fear-based, negative decisions from my past.

My sub-personality that wants this book published is the part I call my "Free Inner Child." This is the part of me that is positive and courageous, the part that sees a "green light" and goes after what it desires.

Another one of my sub-personalities, however, which I call my "Scared Inner Child," (which represents all fears and negative thoughts and is only concerned about my survival), sees a "red light" and puts the brakes on.

Continuing with my story as an example, my painful past-life experiences caused my "Scared Inner Child" to decide that it was not safe for me to help people on a broad scale. If I had not been able to overcome this fear, my "Scared Inner Child" would have prevented me from presenting this book to the public.

Since you are now reading this published book, you know that I have overcome my fears. I have resolved the issues of my "Scared Inner Child" so that I can allow my "Free Inner Child" to share all the information in this book with you.

You may be wondering how I overcame my fears. I succeeded, as you can, by using the HART process. You now know that all of us make negative decisions based on our past experiences. The way we can succeed is to release the old, painful experiences, and then create new positive experiences so that we can make new decisions.

For example, in order for me to overcome the negative decision that I made when I was exiled in Egypt, I closed my eyes and imagined that I was letting go of that experience. In my mind, I burned it away with a laser beam. Then I changed the scene and saw myself supported and rewarded for helping the other women. With that new experience, I was able to make a new decision: "It is safe for me to help people."

As you become familiar with this process, you will learn to release your perceptions of your past-life events and create new positive experiences. Since you make decisions based upon your experiences, you can easily make new positive decisions based upon imagined experiences. Your unconscious will then respond accordingly.

This is one of the most amazing aspects of your unconscious. It exists only in the present, so it does not know the difference between "actual" memories and things you imagine. You can literally rewrite your past and change your feelings and behavior in the future.

Notice that in the HART process we always release the past negative experience. This is very important. You have to clean out the old before you can put in the new. You need to empty your drawer before you can have room to put in new clothes.

This is not done under hypnosis. Instead, I use a process called Creative Visualization. If you were my client, I would begin by asking you to close your eyes, take a few deep breaths, and imagine that you are someplace where you feel safe. When you feel safe, you are more likely to take risks and face your issues.

Then I would guide you to meet with your Wise Person. We all have an image of a wise person in our subconscious mind. This image symbolizes the intuitive part of us that is all-good, all-knowing, and has all the answers we need. You may also call this image your spiritual part or Higher Self. The Wise Person answers your questions, guides, and protects you.

I would then ask you to visualize or sense the person or issue you are having a problem with. My appropriate questions would help you uncover the underlying cause of your problem—the negative decision you made in the past about yourself, others, or the world. Then I would say, "Go back to the time when you made that negative decision and imagine that you are there now."

When you regress back to the original experience, you would have an understanding of what happened and be able to express your feelings. Then I would suggest that you dissolve the scene with a laser beam and then *create* the scene as you would have liked it to be. When you imagine a positive scene, you would then be able to make a positive decision. As soon as you felt complete and relaxed, I would guide you back to the present issue that you started with. At that point, you would likely be able to resolve it. Once you have a new and positive perspective about yourself and others, either your problems dissipate, or you are rational enough to solve them logically.

This process works very well because visualizations are extremely powerful. I often say, "Close your eyes and see clearly." What you see in your mind's eye is what you really believe. What you believe is what you will act on.

Clients sometimes say, "I have no fears". When I ask them to close their eyes, however, and visualize their concerns, they are amazed at how scared they really are. I then welcome them to the human race and acknowledge them for having the courage to face their feelings.

This is what we all have to do. No matter how mature or how intelligent we are, many of us have fears that are causing us to sabotage ourselves in one or more areas of our lives—our relationships, careers, physical appearance, body weight, prosperity, health, or happiness. The truth is that we are powerful, unlimited beings. We are here to be happy, loving, and successful!

(Excerpted from my e-book: *Past Lives/Present Decisions: A Pathway to Transformation*)

21: *Sal's Story*

"I Have to Be Poor and Alone
If I Want to Develop My Spirituality."

My name is Sal and this is my story. I was brought up in a strict and unquestioning Catholic home. My parents and all six of us kids went to church every Sunday. I even attended Saturday Church classes from the time I was eight until I turned sixteen.

I had learned the concept of sin very well. When I was thirteen years old, I started to have normal sexual desires, but I felt confused. I had been taught to feel guilty about my sexual feelings, even though they felt good.

When I was sixteen years old I started to read books on eastern philosophy. I thought I was a very spiritual person. By the time I was twenty years old, I had a ponytail and a beard. People teased me and said that I looked just like Jesus Christ.

When I was twenty-four years old I became aware of a terrible fear arising in me of turning thirty-three. It took me a while to realize that the reason I was so scared was because I was convinced that when I reached thirty-three I would become Jesus. There was no way I wanted that to happen. That would be too much responsibility, and I definitely did not want to be crucified!

From that day on I cut myself off from my spirituality. I shifted from being a spiritual hippie to being an upper-middle-class, white-shirt-and-tie executive in a billion-dollar corporation. I cut off my ponytail and attracted a nice, stable, and appropriate wife into my life. I put most of my energy into my career and family. I became the All-American man with a big house and two cars in the driveway.

From the outside I looked very successful. But internally I felt out of balance and unhappy. My stress level was incredibly high. Fortunately, my beautiful little daughter helped me to relax a little. It is uncanny how children can remind you of how to play and just "be."

For some reason, I kept piling on more and more responsibility. Maybe it was because I was the oldest of six children, and I had learned early in life that I had to be responsible. I never had a chance to be a kid.

After I had been married for three years, I had an affair. Maybe it was my way of playing. My wife found out, and I felt terrible about it. I never meant to hurt her like that, at least not consciously.

I felt I had to talk to someone about my guilt feelings, so I confided in my massage therapist. She recommended that I call Helene to help me work through my confusion. I knew that I needed help, so I made an appointment and went to see her. After a few weeks of therapy with Helene I was able to let go of my lover, even though it was very difficult.

My wife also went to see Helene because she was having difficulty conceiving another child. Through the HART process, she succeeded in overcoming her unconscious fears about becoming pregnant again. Soon after, my wife and I were happy, expectant parents. We were amazed to find out how much our unconscious fears affect us, even to the point of preventing pregnancy.

Our precious little son made our family complete. I should have been very happy, but I was miserable. All the accomplishments seemed to only burden me with even more responsibilities. We bought a larger house than I could afford, so I took on more work. I was the youngest Quality Controller and Production Manager in the company, and I had more work than I could ever possibly keep up with.

You would think that I already had enough responsibilities—but no, not me. I proceeded to get involved with still another lady—this time it was a poor woman who had two small children. I felt that she desperately needed me.

Most people thought I was an extremely responsible person. Yet I had a hidden irresponsible side to my personality. I acted out this secret by having this second extra-marital relationship and by using alcohol and cocaine to excess. At work, 175 people looked to me for guidance, leadership, and moral direction. They did not know that I was snorting cocaine in my office. I was screaming with irresponsibility.

I spent a lot of time and energy trying to be the perfect model—the perfect boss, perfect husband and father, and perfect lover for my girlfriend. But no matter how hard I tried, I still felt imperfect and not good enough. I was always afraid that I would get caught and was terrified that people would find out that I was really an imposter.

My fears kept me in a chronic state of anxiety. I was an extremely tense person. Massage and swimming kept me going, but I still had insomnia. I was thirty-one years old and my life was falling apart. First I started having problems with my girlfriend. One day I managed to forget where to meet her and arrived an hour late. I realized then that I was being passive aggressive. I was angry with her for not "being there" for me. I was also angry with my wife for the same reason.

But the truth was that I really was not angry with them. It was my mom who was the real target of my anger. With six kids in the family, she had hardly been there for me at all. I logically understood that she did her best at the time, but I still felt an insatiable need for women in my life. I could not seem to get enough nurturing.

I needed a lot of sex and was very active with both my wife and lover, but it usually was not satisfying. It was like an addiction, and I kept needing another "fix." I always hoped that the good feeling from the orgasm would last longer, but it never did.

Then my life started falling apart. My marriage was failing; my girlfriend began to make more demands on me, and my corporation eliminated my position. All of a sudden "Mister Perfect" was getting a divorce and had joined the unemployment lines. In desperation, I called Helene for an appointment.

The therapy helped me with my immediate crisis, and I began coping better with my life. After a few sessions, we agreed to explore the reasons why I created such disasters. Helene said, "Sal, close your eyes and go back to the time you made a decision about

143

responsibility." My eyes immediately started to twitch like crazy. I could not see anything but blackness. I knew I was too scared to see.

To help me feel safer, Helene suggested that I imagine sitting in a movie theater with my Wise Person to protect me. Then she asked me to say, "I am willing to see on the movie screen an image of the time when I made a decision about responsibility." All the muscles in my body immediately tensed up when I saw a soldier whom I knew was me.

I was a tall, broad-shouldered Roman soldier standing on guard. When I looked down, I saw my leather breeches. I could see thatched straw huts in the distance. All of a sudden I had a horrible feeling in the pit of my stomach because I realized what had happened. In order to be with a woman, I had deserted my post. While I was gone my unguarded comrades were killed. I was overcome with shame and guilt.

From that experience, I had decided that I am an irresponsible person. I desperately wanted to change that decision, so I burned that one away and visualized a new scene. First I told the soldier that I forgave him for his wrongdoing. Then I visualized my comrades safe from harm because I was doing a good job of guarding them.

As I experienced the new scene, my muscles began to relax. Then I was able to make a new decision: "I am a responsible person." However, I still felt incredibly exhausted and drained. Helene said, "Sal, allow yourself to visualize a rope in front of you that extends to the left, back to your past. The rope has a knot on it representing every lifetime in which you decided that you were irresponsible. How many knots are you seeing?" Almost immediately, I visualized over twenty-five knots. More than ready to release those lifetimes, I imagined that I was burning them away with a laser beam. It took a while, but finally my mental movie screen was clear. I spontaneously took a deep breath and felt relieved, but I still felt tired.

When Helene asked what color represented healing energy to me, I replied "Yellow." Then I imagined that the sun was shining and the bright yellow color was helping me heal and re-energize. I took several deep breaths and watched the yellow color flow through every cell in my body. I felt much better.

When I opened my eyes, I told Helene that I was very skeptical about past lives. Yet I could not deny my body's strong reactions. Helene told me, "Your mind can deceive you, but your body can not. You feel your emotions in your physical body." I sure felt mine. I realized that even if I did not really have past lives, there was obviously a strong decision in my unconscious that affected my life today.

It was no wonder that I did not allow myself to have a fulfilling sex life. I was still punishing myself for going off with a woman and leaving my post! That past-life regression also gave me insight about why I took on so much responsibility. I had to keep proving to myself and to others that I really was responsible. I also believed that if I were not responsible, people would get hurt. So I drove myself to be super-responsible, which resulted in my eventually becoming super-irresponsible, which was a self-fulfilling prophecy.

With my new awareness and my new belief in my responsibility, I began to feel less internal pressure to keep proving myself. I accepted the responsibility for having created the situation of being laid off from my job. The truth was that the demands of the position were killing me. I vowed never to let myself get into that type of "no-win" situation again.

Four months later, I was hired by a medium-size company to do their marketing. I am very happy in my new job. I do not have anyone to "take care of" and I love it.

Helene also helped my wife through her problems, and we have a civilized relationship again. Even though we are divorced, we are communicating well and are equally sharing the responsibilities of parenthood.

About the same time I started my new job, I was able to release my unnecessary feelings of responsibility for my lover and her children. I do not want a needy relationship anymore, so I started to date more independent women.

Ironically, my ex-wife is basically very independent. However, when I was with her, I felt the need to be needed. Since I have overcome many of my old issues and have raised my self-esteem, I no longer desire to be needed. I must admit that my male ego still enjoys it once in a while.

I thought it would be a good idea to attend group therapy because there were still some issues I wanted to resolve, especially in my relationships. I thought it would be helpful to work them out in a co-ed situation.

As Helene worked with the other clients, I was amazed to hear how many of the men and women had issues that were similar to mine. I thought that I was the only one on this earth who suffered. As Helene says, "We are unique, but our problems are not."

One day, when it was my turn to work in the group, Helene asked me to see an image of each of my four parts (mind, body, emotions, and spirit), and to check out whether I was in balance. The image of my mind was a very healthy-looking brain. My body looked fine. Swimming three to five miles a week was keeping me in good shape. My emotions looked like those of a scared little child. I knew that I had to express my feelings more, especially my fears. When it came to the spiritual part, I saw nothing.

Helene suggested that I open up to my spiritual part so that I could be balanced and reach new levels of aliveness and success. I took her advice and attended a New Thought Church called The Church of Religious Science. I liked what they were teaching, and it felt good to me. But I also felt scared. Being a logical person, that did not make sense to me at all.

At my next group therapy session, I told Helene about my fears. She asked me to close my eyes and go back to the time I had made a decision about my spirituality. Immediately my eyes began to flutter uncontrollably. Then she guided me into a movie theater where I was sitting in the back row with my Wise Person; that made me feel more detached and safer. My eyes began to relax.

As the projector rolled, I saw an image on the screen of a desert somewhere in the Middle East. I was wearing an old, dirty, long, gray and white striped robe that also covered my head. I was journeying barefoot, and I lived in poverty in a quest for spirituality.

Then I saw myself looking through the window of a house made out of mud. The family inside looked happy, and I was envious of their life. I then decided that if being spiritual meant living a life of drudgery and being alone with no family or home, I did not want any part of it.

To change that decision, I saw myself as a decently dressed Arab living happily with my wife and children in our comfortable home. I was also a very spiritual person. Then I visualized myself in my present lifetime having all that I want, and being spiritual at the same time. I felt a tremendous sense of relief.

When I opened my eyes I told the group that I now understood why I was afraid to follow a spiritual path. Buried in my unconscious was the belief that I would have to be a poor, lonely nomad, and I would have to give up all my material things as well as my family and lovers. That was certainly reason enough to be scared of spirituality and to want to bury that part of me.

Since that past-life experience, I have returned to the loving Church of Religious Science and now attend regularly. I enjoy the people and the philosophy. The positive reinforcement of my Godliness that I receive helps me grow as a spiritual and emotional being.

I am now thirty-three years old and I feel that I am the Christ, as I thought I would be long ago, but it is different now. I have learned to focus on his resurrection rather than his crucifixion, which was all part of the divine plan. Now I understand that Christ is my proof that I can be 100% conscious of my Godhood in this life. As I become more conscious, I take on more of his attributes, his unconditional love, and healing power. He is an example that I can understand. Like him, I can create anything in my life. I am on my spiritual path, and I now have an abundance of love, joy, and prosperity.

(Excerpted from my e-book: *Past Lives/Present Decisions: A Pathway to Transformation*)

22: *Kate's Story*

"If I Am Too Powerful, I Will Get Killed."

During one of my counseling sessions, Helene had asked me to close my eyes, relax, and imagine that I was entering a long tunnel. Walking through the dark tunnel was scary, so I imagined that my Wise Person was walking with me, and I surrounded myself with white light for protection. Helene had taught me to do that whenever I was scared. When I reached the other end of the tunnel, it was light, and I knew that I was in a past life in Massachusetts during the witch-hunts.

My long dark hair was tangled over my thin shoulders and I was wearing a dirty smock. Many other women and I were huddled together in fear in a dark and dingy prison cell.

Suddenly, I was in a courtroom. Lots of men were staring at me with angry faces and were accusing me of witchcraft. They said I was evil. Terrified, I put my hands over my face and sobbed uncontrollably. They showed no mercy. The angry mob dragged me outside and hung me from my neck alongside three other condemned witches.

This past-life regression helped me understand why I can't wear anything close to my neck in this life, and why I avoid crowds and live in a rural area away from most people. It also helped to explain one reason why I hide behind sixty pounds of fat, and why I am a loner and a perpetual student. I feel safe in the classroom as a follower. I have always avoided being a leader at all costs, even though I am capable of leadership.

Sometimes my husband asks me what I want to do, and I tell him that I do not know. I want to do everything, but I end up doing nothing. To tell you the truth, I realize now that I feel safe doing nothing. That way I cannot displease people, and they are not likely to hurt me.

When I was condemned as a witch, I decided that it was not safe for me to be who I am, a psychic healer. Through therapy, I realized that I am very powerful, intuitive, and psychic. When I compulsively over-ate, I often felt like I was going to burst. One of the things I was stuffing down was the fear of my psychic ability.

Even though I experienced the terror of being hung as a witch, I felt this was the time to come out of hiding and express myself. But first, my Scared Inner Child, who is concerned about my survival, had to believe that I would be safe. So I closed my eyes, visualized the witch hunters, and expressed all my feelings. I yelled and screamed at them because I was furious and terrified. I cried to release my hurt and sadness.

When I felt relaxed, I changed the scene. My new image was of the same men in front of me, but this time they were listening with respect and admiration. They appreciated my psychic and healing abilities and thanked me for all my help. My body relaxed even more, and I felt safe. From that new experience I was able to make a new decision: "I am beginning to believe that it is safe for me to be me."

After that past-life regression, I began to open up more to my intuition. It helped me decide what gifts to buy for other people and even which classes to take. Whenever I asked myself a question, I knew I had made the right choice when I had a feeling of calmness in my abdomen. I guess that is what people refer to as the sixth sense.

It is interesting that I have always known that I was a very powerful. In my teens, I read many books on metaphysics. Meditation was one of my daily activities. I used to say, "I am one with God." The thought occurred to me that perhaps I was being egotistical. People looked at me as if I was strange. When I expressed those words to them, it became obvious to me that I could not talk about these feelings if I wanted to be accepted.

When I was twenty-one years old, I felt an incredible pull to relocate to California and moved there from the East Coast. Even though I had come for a purpose, I stopped meditating and avoided metaphysical books. I married a tall, handsome man and gained sixty pounds.

My husband, George, had been having some problems, and a friend referred him to Helene. After his first session, he urged me to make an appointment. I was reluctant but did call her. My marriage was rocky and I knew I had to do something.

In our first session, Helene guided me to my Scared Inner Child, the part of me that harbored all of my fears—boy, was my child terrified! I imagined she was the stuffed animal that Helene had laid on my chest, and I comforted her. If felt so good to hold her close and tell her she was okay, and that I was going to take care of her from now on.

I had tears in my eyes because I was so sad for all the years she was so frightened and felt so alone. As I began to feel safe, the tension in my stomach eased, and my body relaxed. My Scared Child smiled; the look of terror was no longer on her face.

Then Helene guided me to my Inner Wise Person. She explained that it is the part of me that has all my answers, that comes from love instead of fear. I started to recall all the things I had read in my teen years, including my beliefs about being One with God.

The feeling that I was a powerful Goddess reawakened within me. Helene reassured me that I was not being egotistical, and that we are all powerful and One with God. What a relief! When I now say these words, I experience a wonderful knowingness, and I feel peacefully powerful. I could not wait to return home and share with George what I had learned.

Closing my eyes and checking in with my Scared Inner Child became a daily activity. One morning she told me that she was scared she was evil. At my next counseling session, Helene guided me back to the time when I decided that I was evil. Almost immediately, I visualized a scene in Egypt. It looked like I was in a position of power—somewhat like Cleopatra. I felt very majestic as I saw a great army standing before me, waiting for my command.

I was surprised to recognize George as one of the soldiers. Then it became clear to me that we had a love affair. I had become pregnant and had given birth to a baby girl. Our love affair was discovered. George was killed. He was not supposed to be involved with me. No wonder I tend to push him away in this life. I am afraid if he gets close to me, he will be hurt again.

I felt extremely powerful and excited as I saw myself ordering my troops out to battle. I knew I was sending them to commit mass murder. When Helene asked me what I was deciding about myself, I replied, "When I am powerful, I am evil. I cause many people pain and death."

Since I was more than ready to change that belief, I imagined that I was using a white laser beam to burn away those negative images. Then I visualized myself telling my army that they were free. I told them to go around the countryside and help people. I encouraged them to act in a loving way, to create peace in their own lives, and to assist others.

Then I forgave myself for sending the soldiers to war. From that experience of forgiveness I was able to make a new decision, "I am beginning to believe that I use my power in constructive ways." At that point I began to let go of one of my major fears—that I am an evil person.

I also changed the past life scene with George. I imagined myself being with him. A smile came over my face, and I relaxed as I saw the two of us being married and living happily together. Maybe now I will be able to let George get closer to me, because I can believe that it is safe for him to be with me.

In still another past-life regression I went back to a scene in India. I was a tall man of average build with black hair, dark eyes, and a scruffy beard. My dirty white turban and robe made me look older than my twenty-eight years. Suddenly I put my hands over my eyes. When Helene asked me what I did not want to see, I hesitated. Then I told her that I was a rapist hiding behind an adobe-like building. From that experience I had once again decided that I was a bad person.

I wanted to change that scene as quickly as possible, so I visualized the women I had raped, told them that I was sorry, and asked for their forgiveness. Then I forgave myself. Finally, I imagined myself clean-shaven and being very loving and gracious to women. My new decision was, "I am a good person."

That particular past-life regression helped me pin down another reason why I had a weight problem. I was afraid I would be raped if I were to become thin and very attractive. I also realized that I had a secret desire to be violated and to be a victim. Maybe a part of me felt as though I deserved it.

I had another awareness from experiencing my past life as a man. In this present life, I have often felt tough and masculine. Because of these feelings I thought I might be a lesbian, even though my sexual desires were exclusively for men. I was confused.

This past life showed me that I do indeed have a masculine side, and that I do not have to be afraid of it. In fact, I want to explore it and feel that it is okay. Helene taught me that my feminine side, or right brain, represents my feelings, creativity, and intuition. My masculine side, or left brain, represents my logical and functional part. I am now beginning to feel more at peace with my left brain. I am no longer confused, and my sexuality is not an issue for me anymore.

From what I understand, many men, because of their upbringing, operate from their left brains most of the time. They often do well in their careers, but their relationships are a disaster. A balanced person is a "switch hitter" in knowing when and how to operate from the appropriate part of the brain. Healthy relationships depend greatly on sharing feelings, which are processed in our right brain.

Conversely, many women are programmed not to use their left brain enough, which causes them great difficulty in their careers. I certainly fit into this category. As my therapy progressed, it became clear to me how important it is to open up to my functional, logical mind and to stop playing a "dumb blonde" role.

I also learned that we select our parents to help us learn the lessons we have chosen for this incarnation. It is no coincidence that I picked a mother who blocked her left brain, who never worked, and who chose to be very dependent upon my father, just as I have become dependent on my husband. I guess I needed a model so I could learn how to play the role of a weak and incapable woman.

Actually, both my parents encouraged me to remain a child and never grow up. They overprotected me. Even though I moved three thousand miles away and was married, they still treated me like a little girl.

Now that I have processed through many past lives, I can understand that I set up my present family scenario because of my fear of hurting people with my power and my fear of being hurt because of my abilities. After all, if I feel powerless, I will not be demonstrating abilities like psychic powers that some people may not like. I also will not be directing people in ways that could result in them or others being hurt.

It is a wonderful feeling to understand who I am, what I have been doing, and why. Now I have the choice to play a different role, if I wish, and to become an independent, outgoing, and expressive person.

Working through these past lives has also helped me feel much lighter. Since I feel safer, I am beginning to come out from behind my "wall of fat." I have joined a weight training class and I am more conscious of why I overeat.

I still have some problems, but my relationship with George has improved tremendously. Since we have more insight and clarity about our relationship and ourselves, we have been able to quickly let go of our negative behaviors. We are also aware of how easy it is to fall into old and familiar destructive patterns. We consciously keep working to stay on our new, constructive paths, individually and as a couple.

As far as my career is concerned, I am becoming clearer and more focused on what I want to do. I am even thinking about starting a small business, which will require me to use my left brain more, but I am still not sure what form it will take.

For the first time, I am taking a leadership role and exploring my options in life, all by myself. I am not depending on any other person, class, or teacher, to give me what I need. Of course, I am scared of the unknown, since I have never done this before. But I have a deep, gut feeling that I can be strong, independent, and successful. It is part of my power to believe that I am safe, capable, and a good person. I truly am, and I know that now. Ever since I released the belief that I am evil, I have been able to resume reading metaphysical and spiritual books. I am now feeling much more one with God.

In reviewing my past, I realize that I had stopped working on my spirituality when I arrived in California in 1977 to live with my boyfriend. Before that I was "on the path," which means to me that I felt one with God. I got off the path because I unconsciously thought that living with a man meant that I was sinful and evil. I felt that I did not deserve to be one with God. Now I am feeling a lot less guilty, and I do not feel bad anymore. I remind myself every day that I am a good person, and that I deserve to feel one with God.

It has been marvelous to learn that God loves us all unconditionally, and that we do not need to ask for his forgiveness. We are the only ones who need to do any forgiving. We need to forgive ourselves. God wants us to do whatever we need to do in order to feel good and to be holy, which is our natural state. When we feel spiritual, loving, powerful, and unlimited, we can do what we really came here to do. That is to bring His unconditional love to this earth plane, to feel One with ourselves and each other, and to realize that we are all sisters and brothers, Children of God. Then, and only then, will we have world peace.

(Excerpted from my e-book: *Past Lives/Present Decisions: A Pathway to Transformation*)

23: *Spiritual Affirmations*

Many essential and empowering insights and solutions are shared in this book. I am also including loving, positive, spiritual thoughts, known as affirmations. These can help you on your pathway to love and enlightenment.

I suggest that you read, say or sing these truths until they become part of your automatic thinking. It is helpful to include your name to personalize the affirmations. If you find that you are not able to accept the divine thought(s), add the words, "beginning to." For example: "I, Helene, love myself," becomes, "I, Helene, am beginning to love myself."

1. I accept that God, the creator and essence of everything, loves me.

2. I am honored and privileged to be here now on Planet Earth. I came here wholly by choice to experience life to the fullest.

3. I am here to be my precious divine self.

4. I am like nature, totally accepting and simply being.

5. I accept that because God loves me and gave me free will.

6. I accept that God has given me the power to create whatever I desire.

7. I believe that what I do and say does make a difference.

8. I am speaking and acting from my heart.

9. I am the designer and master of my life.

10. I am communing with God in all that I do, when I am being loving and joyful.

11. I am following my path of joy.

12. I am only doing what makes me happy and excited.

13. I am living in the now and having fun.

14. I believe that my destiny is to be happy and joyful.

15. I have unlimited thinking which is drawing to me whatever I desire.

16. I am letting go of any thoughts that deny my power and magnificence.

17. I believe that this is an abundant and loving universe.

18. I am worthy of receiving all that I desire.

19. I am seeing money as another way of giving and receiving.

20. I am accepting that prosperity is my birthright.

21. I am asking for what I want and allowing myself to receive it.

22. I am directing my mind to carry out the ideas of my spirit.

23. I accept that everything I think, I will feel and manifest.

24. I am following my heart, my dreams, and my desires.

25. I have patience and faith that everything is in divine order.

26. I am the only one who truly knows what is best for me.

27. I am totally responsible for all that I have experienced.

28. I have the freedom to choose my thoughts.

29. I am listening inside myself for my truths.

30. I am listening to my intuition, which is my inner wisdom.

31. I am asking myself daily, "What can I do to experience and express love?"

32. I believe that everything I have done has made me the magnificent being I am today.

33. I realize that all my choices were right and necessary for my growth.

34. I accept that the only thing I have done wrong was to believe that I have done wrong.

35. I am loving and nurturing my physical body, the temple of my soul.

36. I am offering my body healthy foods, prepared and eaten with love.

37. I accept my chosen body and I see its beauty and magnificence.

38. I accept that my negative beliefs cause my illnesses and accidents.

39. I am healing my body by releasing my negative thoughts and loving myself.

40. I am allowing myself to feel all my emotions.

41. I am choosing my responses to my feelings.

42. I am accepting that fear is an illusion.

43. I have the courage to face my fears.

44. I am acknowledging and releasing all my fears and judgments.

45. I am overcoming my addictions and resolving my conflicts.

46. I am looking to see what other people are mirroring for me when I am upset.

47. I am exploring what I need to do to remember that I am love and I have it all.

48. I believe that everything I have done has made me the magnificent being I am today.

49. I realize that all my choices were right and necessary for my growth.

50. I accept that the only thing I have done wrong was to believe that I have done wrong.

51. I am loving and nurturing my physical body, the temple of my soul.

52. I am offering my body healthy foods, prepared and eaten with love.

53. I accept my chosen body and I see its beauty and magnificence.

54. I accept that my negative beliefs cause my illnesses and accidents.

55. I am experiencing self-love—the key to my health, happiness, and godliness.

56. I believe that when I love myself, I am loving God.

57. I am taking the responsibility to love myself.

58. I am loving myself no matter how I feel and what I do.

59. I am loving and accepting myself unconditionally.

60. I am depending on myself to fulfill all my needs.

61. I am falling in love with life and myself.

62. I am only powerful when I love myself.

63. I am allowing universal love to flow through me.

64. I am looking in the mirror every day and saying, "I love you."

65. I am a generator of love.

66. I am my own best friend and teacher.

67. I am only following the teachings of unconditional love.

68. I am a model for many people how to simply be.

69. I have everything inside of me to make me happy.

70. I am finding my love and security inside of me.

71. I am measuring my success each day by how much I have loved.

72. I am radiating with self-love and attracting loving people to me.

73. I am being the person I want my partner to be.

74. I am primarily with my loved one to learn unconditional love.

75. I am with my loved one for the joy of sharing what I already have.

76. I am focusing on the essence, love, and not the form, the relationship.

77. I am acknowledging my sexuality and directing it in a positive way.

78. I am seeing sexual union as another way to give and receive love.

79. I feel one with God when I allow myself to feel one with my partner.

80. I see God in everyone; all are my brothers and sisters—we are one family.

81. I am allowing myself to be all that I am.

82. I am an androgynous spirit--male and female.

83. I accept that everyone is equal in the eyes of God.

84. I am feeling compassion for the pain that people have chosen for their soul growth.

85. I am patient and accepting that we all grow at our own pace.

86. I understand that we all express our truth as we perceive it.

87. I am seeing the beauty in everyone and everything.

88. I believe that everyone is linked together through the grace and love of God.

89. I am surrendering to my spirituality and embracing my godliness.

90. I feel my divine parent, God, is always with me.

91. I am one with God, and God is one with me.

92. I am looking in the mirror and seeing God the creator.

93. I know that my will is God's will; we are one.

94. I love as God loves, unconditionally.

95. I am God-Man/Woman expressing divine perfection on this planet.

96. I am becoming enlightened; that is, lighting up and loving all of me.

97. I am a light for many others to follow.

98. I am my own savior.

99. I am here on earth to reclaim my godliness.

100. I accept that now is the time for my transformation.

101. I believe that the way home is on the wings of love.

102. I am humbly feeling my divine holiness.

103. I am feeling inner peace, my greatest contribution to world peace.

104. I accept that peace, love, and joy are now filling this blessed planet.

105. I am like the wind, powerful, free and ongoing.

106. I am a brilliant white light illuminating the universe.

107. I am whole and complete.

108. I am returning to my greatness and my glory.

109. I am an ongoing spirit. I am forever.

DEAR GOD

Please help me...

Remember that you are always with me.

Accept that I'm worthy of your love and support.

Understand that you love me no matter what I think, say or do.

Learn how to be as patient with myself as you are with me.

Forgive myself when I blunder, and learn from my mistakes.

Be grateful for all that I have and all that I can do.

Love and appreciate my mind, body, spirit, and emotions.

Accept that prosperity is my birthright.

Feel lovable and good enough so that I can allow others to love me.

Realize that I have the power to create what I want in my life, and that I deserve to be happy, healthy and successful.

Thank you for always listening and guiding me. I love you!

PLEASE GOD

Please help me...

Remember that you are always with me.

Accept that I'm worthy of your love and support.

Understand that you love me no matter what I think, say, or do.

Learn how to be patient with myself as you are with me.

Forgive myself when I blunder, and learn from my mistakes.

Be grateful for all that I have and all that I can do.

Love and appreciate my mind, body, spirit, and emotions.

Accept that prosperity is my birthright.

Feel lovable and good enough so that I can allow others to love me.

PART III

Messages from the Light

24: *Mission Possible*

The Arcturians, from the star Arcturus, have helped me in every area of my life. They came to me in August 1992 and since then have been helping me and serving others through me. They are the most evolved ETS from the fifth dimension, which is pure love (no fear). They asked me to write the book about my experiences with them, "The Arcturians Speak! My Life with Loving ETS".

They are known as the "Cosmic Doctors of the Universe" and have often taken me up on their ship to help me heal and rejuvenate. As they requested, I have also guided many individuals and groups onto their ship. People have reported amazing experiences. I even guided a client up with her dog and they both were in the same healing room. I understand that the mind has a hard time with this concept because it only understands what is physical and not metaphysical (beyond the physical). It is an undeniable experience, however, for the participant. People often report a deep level of love, peace, and healing, as the Arcturians beam love and light energy through them.

These evolved ETS honored me with the title of "Arcturian Ambassador." I am grateful to serve in this way and be a bridge for them and many people on earth. They also helped me channel their healing, high vibration tones and the "Universal Language of the Light." I have presented them many times and recorded a CD with world-known Steven Halpern, "Healing Sounds from Arcturus." More information is in the appendix.

The dear, loving Arcturians have helped me immeasurably to actualize my divine mission, and they continue to do so. Each day I have more confidence that my dreams are becoming realities, that I can be all that I am and do all that I came to do in ease, grace, love, and joy.

All the wonderful experiences I have had with the Arcturians and other guides from the light have reassured me that my mission of reaching as many people as I can to "love themselves to peace" is possible. I have more confidence and faith that I have all the help I need from this earth plane and above. I do need, however, to continue to overcome any fears that block me, to listen to and follow my intuition, and to be patient and trusting since everything flows in divine time.

I felt honored when the Arcturians, Mother Mary and Sananda (the spirit of Jesus) asked me to include their loving, channeled messages in the last part of this book. They have been helping me evolve, as well as offering many people profound healings through me, even over the telephone. Their goal is to leave you, the reader, in a loving, high state of being.

I am totally committed to actualizing my true self, my divine spirit, on this magnificent Planet Earth – to follow my spirit with no hesitation. I realize that I am a spiritual being who chose to be here to have a human experience. I am now ready to walk forward into the unknown with ease, grace, love, and light because I trust that my spirit knows the future.

It is now time to hear the Arcturians speak. It is an excerpt from their channeling in the book, "Arcturians Speak." I suggest that you read their words with all your senses. Allow yourself to feel their love and light, and let them speak to your heart and your spirit. Open up to their divine wisdom and enjoy the experience. May their message touch you as it has touched many others, including me.

It has been a joy to share these pathways to love and enlightenment. May this book assist you to live spirituality, and to believe that your divine mission is also possible. May it help you actualize your soul growth and assist you to move forward on your divine path with ease and grace, joy and abundance, and love and light.

Namaste! (I honor the divine in you!)

25: *Arcturians Speak*

Greetings, dear one, we are the Arcturians. We are from the fifth dimension and we are of the light. We are very grateful and honored to be with you now. We wish to share some of our thoughts and feelings with you many beautiful earthlings on planet Earth.

We came here many eons ago to settle this planet, and then we evolved to the fifth dimension. So we know what it is like, dear one, to live on Planet Earth. Although we must say that it wasn't as "civilized," as you call it, as it is now. But we lived here; we bred here, learned here, and worked here. We have much compassion for you now as we know and understand much that you endure. That is one reason why we agreed to come when God requested our appearance. We came to assist you at this time as we had been assisted when we went through this transformation.

We are beings of the light. What does that mean, dear one? That means that we do not have fear controlling us, or guilt or resentment, or anger or even sadness. We see clearly, as there are no more illusions up here in our dimension. We see everything as light. There is nothing of darkness. We see that we are all one with God and we are all one with each other. There are no doubts and there are no concerns, as we can see the divine truth in front of us, and all around us and inside of us. We see the truth. We see the wisdom of the universe. We see the divinity of all there is.

We are facing a new eon, a new time, dear one, beautiful, Earth being. Earth is evolving and becoming a star and it is time for you to graduate. It is time for Earth to graduate into its brilliant star. It no longer wants to play the game of darkness and light. There will be other planets that will accommodate those who still wish to play this game or wish to grow in that way.

You are never alone. There are many beings on this planet you can call your sisters and brothers as you are all one family. You can also call on us beings from the stars. We are your family, too. We are all brothers and sisters of the divine source. So therefore, we are all part of the divine source; every single one of you, no matter what you have done.

You can now recall who you are. And you can forgive yourself if you feel you need to. You never need forgiveness, dear one, from the beings from the light. But if you feel you need to do that, then forgive yourself.

Forgive others for their ignorance of who they really are; for their forgetting. Know that they are a mirror for you. You have forgotten too, or you would not be in pain. Or, if they did something that disturbed you, you would simply know that they were just acting out the illusion. That is not who they are. That is not any reflection of who you are. You are divine light no matter what people say or do. You are what you are and nothing can change that.

You cannot change a rock into water. A rock remains a rock and water remains water. So whether it may be in a different form, whether it is a rock that is sculpted, or whether the water is in the form of a waterfall, or a creek that is flowing, or a creek that is stagnant, it is all water or rock. You are all light, you are all love, you are all peace and joy, and your spirit lives forever.

When you choose to leave, dear one, your body will no longer be needed. Your body will return to its elements on Mother Earth, which is what it is made of. And your spirit will be released and soar back into the light. It will soar because spirits always soar. They don't have any limitations. They don't need to learn how to fly. They know, because that is who they are. And you are all evolved spirits from many different higher dimensions, here again to play the game called life on Earth as a human being.

We want to reassure you, dear one, that this is not an easy place to be. We know that and we know why it is attractive. Many lessons have come to you here. You have much courage to be on Earth. There are many places to be in the galaxy and in the universe. But you have chosen to be here in whatever form you are because of your free will. And you can choose at any time to be another way on this planet, another way of being.

167

And you can also choose to leave. And it is not bad when you leave. It is something to be celebrated, as you are leaving the illusion. So we want to reassure all you beloved people that are mourning your loved ones who chose to release themselves back into the universe. Yes, your personality is missing them. And we understand that from our hearts. But we also want you to know that you can always speak to them. You can always connect with them because you are both spirits. Just pick up the "telephone." Allow them to come to you. Talk to them; they are always with you--always. You are never apart.

Now that we have spoken about who you are, dear one, we would like to tell you who we are. We are light beings also referred to as ETS. We serve in conjunction with many other beings of the light. We are like one NATO with many different light beings serving together as a cosmic team. We come from many universes and galaxies. In this one united force we keep peace on Planet Earth and we keep peace in the universe.

We are honored and grateful to be with you and to serve you. We have been honored and grateful to be able to serve this being who we are speaking through now. We would be honored and grateful to serve you too – if that is what you have asked for before you came into this incarnation, or if at any time you choose to ask us now. But we cannot do anything, dear one, unless you ask, because we totally honor your free will. We will never, never disregard your free will. You see dear one, it is most difficult to do that from this plane, as we know that we will take on your pain and your Karma. We do not want to experience that. We are complete with pain.

There is another reason why we will not dishonor or ignore your free will. Because we love you unconditionally for the highest good of all, we would never inflict our wishes on you. And let us say, dear one, as a side comment, that this is one way that you know that you love someone unconditionally. You would only do everything to support them in doing whatever their free will wishes them to do. You will not rescue them. You will not take care of them. But you will help them to become who they are – who their divine presence is – whether they are with you or not. Whether or not they are doing what you like, you are totally in support of them being who they came here to be.

Now, dear one, let's get back to us beings called the Arcturians. We have many, many ships in your sky. You cannot all see them, although some of you do. We can choose for you to see our ships or not, because we have the ability, as you do also when you are on other planes, to dematerialize and materialize at the blink of an eye. We will be coming here in great masses to help you remember who you are. We are not here to scare you as some of the movies are expressing. We are here to help you – to serve you.

Remember, dear one, that love is your power; light is your power. Fear makes you powerless. So release your fears. Drop them into the water. Let them disperse as a drop of ink disperses when it is thrown into the water. The water will transform your fears. Then allow love and light in the form of a color, vibration, or frequency to come through you and fill your divine being, to remind you of who you are.

You will just be an observer, as you know that everyone and everything is acting out this divine game we call polarities – the game played on Planet Earth. And when you all evolve above that, or at least the mass majority, the critical mass as it is said on your planet, earth will be evolving into a star.

And you will be going with it, and you will be living heaven on earth. Imagine a life, dear one, where there is no fear, where there is no struggle. There is only beingness; only love and service to yourself, to your fellow mankind on your planet and others. Can you imagine that?

Seek people, dear one, who are shining their light – not so that you can become their slave or their follower – but so that you can see what they are doing, and allow them to remind you of who you are. But do not be an eternal student, dear one. We cannot advise that. The finest teacher, a master, will give you the tools, the insights, the awareness, and the wisdom, so that you can walk on your own in light and love and spread the word to others. You are here to learn this. You are to graduate and then to teach. And so the process goes on.

You are here temporarily. You are not here to cling to the human experience. You are here to evolve in the human experience; and there is much challenge to that, as you probably know at this time. So shall we say you get many points when you evolve on this Planet Earth? When you shift from fear into love, when *you go back to your home, you go back into higher dimensions and get closer to the divine source.*

We are very grateful, dear one, to be with you. We are very grateful for this being, called Helene, who has allowed us, as we have prearranged with her before this incarnation, to serve through her.

You are all here on a cosmic mission. It has been scary for her in some ways. She, like most beings, did not want to appear weird, or different, or as a freak, or burned again as a witch. It has taken her much to overcome these fears. We have supported her; we have had compassion and helped her in all ways that we could, and she did the rest of the healing.

We cannot do it for you. But we can do it with you. We are always calling you, dear one, but you need to pick up the receiver. God, all the angels and archangels and ETS from the light are always calling you. You are never alone. Pick up the receiver, dear one. Tune into your intuition; open up to divine guidance. Open up to divine love and wisdom and you shall be healthy, prosperous, truly alive, and live in love. We wish you all that we wish ourselves and everyone, which is nothing less than divine love, divine light, divine peace, and joy. Thank you for allowing us to share this with you.

Namaste!

(Excerpts from my e-book, **Arcturians Speak! My Life with Loving ETS**.)

Arcturus (Arc·tu·rus) is a bright orange star about twenty-eight times larger than the Sun, the fourth brightest star in the sky, the brightest star in the constellation Boötes, and approximately thirty-six light-years from Earth. Its name is derived from the Greek and signifies "the Guardian of the Bear". It can be found by extending the curve of the Big Dipper's handle.

26: *Divine Messages from Mother Mary and Sananda*

When I was preparing this book for the publisher, Mother Mary and Sananda asked me to allow them to channel their messages to you. It is always an honor and joy to bring through their divine love, light, and wisdom.

I realized that it was a wonderful last chapter, as we reinforce the divine truth and deepen your feelings of divine love. As mentioned in the Channeling chapter, beings from the eighth dimension or higher have evolved beyond an individual spirit and speak in the "we" form.

I suggest that you open your heart and allow their healing love to flow deep inside of you. You deserve their love! Enjoy this elixir of life!

MESSAGE FROM MOTHER MARY

Dear ones, we love you so much. All that you do is appreciated by us.

All that you are, we divinely respect and honor. All that you think and feel is valuable for your consciousness and that of the planet. You make much more of a difference than you realize. Look not around you to be concerned about anything. Look up always and remember that we are always with you.

We love you unconditionally and will always support your divine life as well as your divine mission. We respect your courage to face your earth challenges, which we see as opportunities for you to expand and reach deep inside of yourself to remember the truth. You are love and light. Only blocking that truth will cause you to be distant from your joy and happiness. Embrace your truth and you will experience magnificent joy that is immeasurable. Can you imagine that, dear one?

We see your struggle on Planet Earth. We see your human predicaments and we have compassion for everyone. We see the rainbow in you as well as around you, even when things appear difficult. We see your light as it shines beyond your human body forever. It is always glowing, even when you are not aware of its magnificence and power to overcome the darkness. As you know, dear ones, the light removes the darkness. Magically, it makes it disappear. Magically it shows you all that there is to see. Not to fear, dear one, but to embrace and love. And when you love, dear one, you cannot feel fear.

Your earth parents loved and still love you, whether or not you are or were aware of this divine feeling. We understand that it may be difficult to believe, based on the lack of evidence. That caused you much pain, dear one, as we all want to be loved.

However, the love was always there from deep inside of them and deep inside of you. The love also was and is always shining down from God, Sananda, and all the angelic beings, including us. Embrace that love, dear one. Allow it into all of your cells, all of your being, to activate the love inside of you.

Dearest one, when you feel that love deep in your being, life will be, as you say on earth, a "bed of roses." Life will be glorious as you will no longer be in the illusion of fear, of doubt, of lack. You will walk forward in confidence and clarity, in joy and abundance. You will treasure every moment and laugh often because of the joy you experience. You will smile at the illusion: the illusion being the parts of you that may at times feel unlovable, inadequate, powerless, or weak. Then, dearest one, you will be able to reassure that inner part that you are very lovable, adequate, powerful, and strong. That is what love does for you and to you. That is your power! That is all there is. Always remember we love you!

Namaste, Mother Mary

MESSAGE FROM SANANDA (THE SPIRIT OF JESUS)

"Dear ones, we are with you. We have always been with you and always will. We never leave you. You are never alone. We have so much love for you that it could fill the entire galaxy and beyond. Feel our love, dear ones. Feel our divine presence. You are worthy of the light!

Allow the light to come down through you and then spread it with your outstretched arms to everyone and everything. That is who and what you are; that is healing and it is your power. That is the way to live in joy, harmony, and peace. We ask that you question no more. Thank the mind for being concerned, and reassure it that you are safe and okay. You are a vibrant child of God. You are one with us. You are magnificent!

Dear one, open your heart and let us in. Come home to the light. Come to the realization that you are home when you are walking and living in the light. Let go of any illusions of suffering, evil, and guilt. There is only light and the absence of light, also known as fear.

Sing with us the glory of God and you. Take your stand with beings of the light. Be in your peace and peace shall prevail. Be in your joy and you will be joyful. Be a divine model for others. Learn the light lesson well and teach it to whoever will listen. Teach not as a taskmaster, not as a detached superior being, but as an equal brother or sister who cares and shares unconditionally. You do not need others to change. You are not dependent on them for your light, for your happiness.

There is much more we can share with you, dear ones. We have chosen instead to express the most important message: the essence of spirituality, the essence of who and what you and we are.

We are your divine Brother. Mother Mary is your divine Sister. We are all loved children of Father God and Mother Goddess. We are all one family. We are here for you and with you. We love you."

Namaste! Sananda

Appendix

The Arcturians Orchestrate a Healing CD

To my surprise, the Arcturians (ETS) joined my angelic team in 1992, five years after I began channeling angelic beings of the light. Following their guidance made my life an even more thrilling, spiritual adventure. One morning I heard in my inner voice, "Visit your friend in Florida for three weeks." It was January 2008, and I was living in Santa Fe, New Mexico. Bernice was thrilled that I was coming, and I was excited to go to a warm climate. I had faith that there was a purpose for me to make this trip, and I trusted that it would all unfold perfectly. The Arcturians had not given me any clues about their amazing project.

When I awoke one morning in sunny Florida, I was surprised to hear these intuitive words, "Your next move is to Marin County, CA." A few days later, Bernice informed me that her friend, Mary, was coming over that night for dinner with her friend, Steven Halpern. He had connected with Mary when she had taught classes in his mother's retirement home.

In the 1980's, Steven Halpern lived in Marin County, and we had met at conferences and gatherings. We were both popular presenters in the San Francisco Bay Area. More than twenty years later, it was wonderful to sit next to him at the dinner table and re-connect. Suddenly, I heard in my inner voice, "Tell him you do sound healing." So I said, "I channel the Arcturians, and they sing healing tones and the Universal Language of the Light through me. I have presented them at conferences."

174

"Great, I would like to hear them," Steven replied. We all proceeded to the living room, and I channeled their high vibration healing sounds. To my surprise, this world famous founder of New Age Music, handed me his business card as he said, "If you ever get to Marin, call me. Maybe we can do something together."

A smile crossed my face. I knew that the Arcturians had something up their sleeves. The synchronicity was too obvious to ignore. I realized all that they had to orchestrate in order for us to re-connect on the East Coast. The angelic guides from the light are miraculous. Life is amazing when we listen and act on their messages.

One month later, when I was back in New Mexico, I heard in my inner ear, "You are to move to Marin in May for five months." I was happy to be going to such a beautiful area for the spring and summer. Once again, I was guided to post what I wanted on a website. A few hours later, I received an email with the message, "I have your perfect place. Please call me."

When I spoke to Susan she informed me that she had to go to the East Coast to take care of her deceased mother's affairs. I could rent the 2,000-square-foot home for the five months she would be away. Thank you, angels! Once again they effortlessly guided me to the perfect place to live and pay rent that was way below the market.

Once I was settled in, I contacted Steven. After another meeting, we agreed to record this divine CD. It was an amazing experience for me. I was always told not to sing because I cannot carry a tune. However, here I was singing with a master musician and being recorded in a professional studio.

Steven and I set our intent to channel the Arcturians' healing sounds. I then told him what the Arcturians called the first piece, "Opening the Heart." He smiled, sat down in front of his keyboard and started playing delightful, heartfelt music. I then surrendered to the Arcturians and allowed them to use my untrained voice to bring through their healing sounds to open the heart.

I will never forget the technician's and the studio owner's reactions. They expressed their amazement. "Wow! I never heard such beautiful, unusual sounds. They are not from this planet!" Their positive feedback helped me believe that this CD would be successful.

I have been a professional therapist, teacher, author, and speaker for more than thirty years, and I have many more goals that include these strengths. However, I never imagined that this CD would be channeled and loved by so many people. The testimonials have been awesome. I am so grateful that Steven and I had the courage to listen to our inner voices and create such a healing, transformational CD.

I want to express my deep gratitude to Steven Halpern for being open to these highly evolved space beings and for co-creating this divine, cosmic CD. I am also extremely appreciative that the Arcturians chose me to be one of their ambassadors, and to bring through their healing sounds that come from a very large crystal on their planet.

It is a wonderful feeling to know that the "Healing Sounds from Arcturus" CD is another way I am fulfilling my mission of helping people to "love themselves to peace," which I believe is the key to health, happiness, success, and world peace. It is exciting, rejuvenating, and so much fun to allow guides to serve through us!

Educational Materials and Services

With the goal of assisting as many people as she can, Helene Rothschild has lectured extensively, and written and recorded the following inspirational, empowering, and self-help educational materials:

"Healing Sounds From Arcturus" CD with Steven Halpern (note the video on YouTube)

Books and E-Books
Reports/Questionnaires
MP3 Audios and CDS

FREE on her website: Inspirational Newsletter, Articles, Poems, Teleconferences, e-booklet, Mp3 audio, and more.

Helene also offers teleconferences, independent studies, Spiritual Masters Trainings, classes in the HART process, workshops, lectures, and international, transformational and healing telephone sessions for you and your pets.

Her services include:

1. Channeled Healings by numerous guides including:

   Sananda (the Spirit of Jesus)
   Mother Mary
   St. Germain
   Kuthumi
   Archangel Michael
   The Arcturians.

2. Body Scan Readings and Healings

3. Chakra Healings

4. Psychic Readings and Healings

5. Guided Healing Visits on the Arcturian Ship

6. Helping you Meet and Channel Your Angelic Guides
   Telepathic "Ghost Busting"

7. Past Life Healings

8. E-Mail Readings

9. Marriage and Family Counseling

More information can be found on her websites:

www.angeloncall.net and www.helenerothschild.com

Or call her message center at 1-888-639-6390, USA

About the Author

Helene Rothschild MS, MA, MFT, Marriage, Family Therapist, was born in Brooklyn, New York, USA. She received a Bachelor and Master's Degree in Science in Health and Physical Education at Brooklyn College, and taught at Lafayette High School for six years.

In 1976, she moved to California and earned a Master's degree in Marriage, Family, and Child Counseling at the University of Santa Clara in Santa Clara, California. After Helene became licensed, she founded and directed the Institute for Creative Therapy, a non-profit educational counseling center. In addition to counseling clients, she trained and supervised other therapists in a process she developed, called Creative Therapy (now called HART—Holistic And Rapid Transformation).

Helene has also shared her unique ideas with hundreds of audiences and facilitated many self-help workshops. She hosted her own local radio and television shows and appeared numerous times in the media, including on the international Cable News Network (CNN).

Helene's mission is to help as many people as she can to "love themselves to peace," which she believes is the key to health, happiness, and success, and the greatest contribution to world peace. She has touched millions of people internationally with her inspirational and self- help articles, books, e-books, CDs, MP3 audios, cards, and posters.

Helene has committed her life to service. She has the courage to listen to and follow her intuition. In 1993, her inner wisdom motivated her to move to Sedona, Arizona. In 1997, she founded and was the CEO of Joyful Living, a non-profit educational organization with the mission to assist people to experience love and peace. Through Joyful Living, she has donated thousands of her educational materials to other non-profit organizations.

In 2003, Helene moved to Carmel Valley, California. In November 2004, her intuition guided her to sell everything and embark on an international spiritual journey. To her surprise, she was guided to live in Australia, California, Hawaii, New Mexico, and Oregon. She also visited and served in Florida, New Zealand, and Puerto Rico. In the spring of 2009, Helene returned to Northern California and continues to help many people through her international phone sessions, classes, workshops, lectures, media appearances, and educational materials.

Helene has raised two children and has five grandchildren. She loves to have fun celebrations, dance, hike, network, and explore different places.

Endorsements for
Helene Rothschild

Helene Rothschild "walks her talk" and is definitely an "Angel on Call"! I highly recommend her for 1:1 private consultation as she works just as fast, gets to the core, and assists in healing whatever is present in the moment to heal any blocks that are there. She wastes no time! She lives in trust and faith with her angels/guides on a daily basis and it shows! ~ **Cynthia**

Helene thank you so much for helping me explore and deepen my channeling. I loved what you offered! ~ **Elsie**

When Helene did a brief energy healing on me at the Channeling event, she said that she removed a black band from my throat. The next day I was unable to smoke cigarettes. The desire was completely gone. The results were pretty awesome! Thank you! ~ **Sarah**

Helene Rothschild is the finest healer I've worked with—and I've worked with many great healers. In her presence, one feels instantly safe, seen, felt, and heard. Because she is a trained Marriage & Family Therapist her analytical prowess is very attuned. She is also incredibly psychic and intuitive. This makes her a powerhouse.

But I think it is Helene's deep belief in the life of the spirit that makes her the transformational healer that she is. Helene LIVES what she teaches. She is bright, grounded, compassionate, straight forward, funny, and very loving. Even though her work is steeped in metaphysics and energy healing, there is nothing woo-woo about her. She's the real thing.

Helene is a devoted, tenacious and very effective healer's healer. I recommend her to anyone who wants to connect fully to the Source and do the real work with joy and a renewed sense of well-being and gratitude. ~ **Simone**

I have been honored to have had many spiritual teachers. In the Spiritual Master's training Helene put it all together for me, with the bigger picture of the world outside our immediate sensory awareness beautifully outlined and explained. She helped me heal old wounds and gain the skills to heal others. And she helped me to tune in to my intuition as a constant practice, which has, well, changed my life. I am deeply grateful to Helene and to my guides who brought me to her door. Namaste! ~ **Brenda**

The Spiritual Master's class was transformational for me. I learned some powerful tools and techniques for clearing negative thoughts and emotions and for tapping into my inner self when making daily decisions. I developed skills for remaining neutral, calm, and inspired when interacting with others both inside and outside of work. ~ **John**

Made in the USA
Las Vegas, NV
28 January 2022

42453196R00105